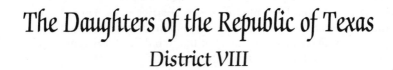

The Daughters of the Republic of Texas
District VIII

Presents

A Pinch of This
and a
Handful of That

Delma Cothran Thames
Editor

EAKIN PRESS Austin, Texas

DISCLAIMER

The home remedies and household hints contained in this book are provided for historical purposes only. No express or implied warranties with regard to their efficacy or safety are made by Daughters of the Republic of Texas, District VIII. Do not use them without first consulting a physician or other appropriate medical professional. Daughters of the Republic of Texas are not engaged in rendering medical advice.

FIRST EDITION
THIRD PRINTING

Copyright © 1988
By the Daughters of the Republic of Texas,
District VIII

Published in the United States of America
By Eakin Press, P.O. Box 23069, Austin, Texas 78735

ISBN 0-89015-649-2

*This book is dedicated
to the memory and spirit of the men and women
who achieved and maintained the independence of Texas.*

The book is published to commemorate two ensuing events:

*Daughters of the Republic of Texas Centennial
1891–1991
and
Lone Star Flag of Texas Sesquicentennial
1839–1989*

A Recipe for a Happy Day

A little dash of water cold,
A little leaven of prayer,
A little bit of sunshine gold,
Dissolved in morning air.
Add to your meal some merriment,
Add thoughts for kith and kin,
And then as a prime ingredient
A plenty of work thrown in.
Flavor it all with essence of love,
And a little dash of play;
Then a nice old book and a glance above
Complete a happy day.

Contents

Acknowledgments

Editor: Delma Thames
District VIII Representative
**Publishing Committee
Cochaired by:**
Carolyn Thurmond and
Frances Underwood
Anna Fell
Lel Hawkins
Betty McAnelly
Jennifer Mellett
Ellagene Stenger
Karen Thompson
Wilena Young
Content Committee:
Marjorie Brandenberger
Myrtle Callan
Alyce Ferguson
Linda Halliburton
Lel Hawkins

Marjorie Hyatt
Rox Ann Johnson
Joyce Moore
Reed Parr
Karen Thompson
Carolyn Thurmond
Frances Underwood
Proofing Committee:
Caroline Bass
Anna Fell
Adena Hardin
Sharon Hardin
Lel Hawkins
Billie Jordan
Betty McAnelly
Ann Pollard
Caroline Ryals
Ellagene Stenger
Frances Underwood

The Daughters of District VIII wish to express our appreciation to the Llano Chapter for submitting the most popular title for our book, and to all who provided chapter illustrations.

The Daughters of District VIII wish to express our gratitude and thanks to all individuals who donated their favorite recipes and helpful hints, and to those who helped with the compiling and the selling or in any other way contributed to the publication of this delightful book.

Foreword

By Liz Carpenter

In Appreciation

In a time of microwave cooking, frozen foods, and pizzas delivered-in-thirty-minutes-or-you-don't-pay, it is with awe and delight that I read *A Pinch of This and a Handful of That*.

This collection of recipes and household hints of our foremothers compiled by the Daughters of the Republic of Texas tells it like it was. You not only cook by it, but get a history lesson and a stretch of the imagination in the process. Every page brings a smile and respect for the pioneer woman.

As one wrote, "Almost any woman can cook well, if she has plenty with which to do it, but the real science of cooking is to be able to cook a good meal, or dish, with little out of which to make it."

Thanks to Eakin Press we now have this delightful, sometimes hilarious insight into life before Texas was a state, told with the wisdoms picked up along the camp trail and over the range.

Take eggs. I got carried away with the information I found on eggs. Writing in 1850, an early daughter or mother of Texas (and she was doubtless both), tells you "How to Get More Eggs — Keep hens quiet and well fed if you wish to fatten them, but make them scratch for their living if you desire eggs." There! It figures, doesn't it?

To choose eggs, "in putting the hand round the eggs, and presenting to the light, the end which is not covered, it should be transparent. if you detect some tiny spots, it is not newly laid, but may be very good for all ordinary purposes except boiling soft." The household hint goes on to tell me something I have always wanted to know about eggs, but was afraid to ask: "The white of a newly-laid egg boiled soft is like milk; that of an egg a day old is like rice boiled in milk; and that of an old egg, compact, tough, and difficult to digest." Supermarket here I come.

I marvel at the early dates of the recipes — Butter Rolls made by Elizabeth James Standifer who settled in Bastrop County in 1827. And grape wine, made in 1840. Mulberry and Cherry Wine followed.

I marvel at the home remedies for "asthma — linseed oil, honey, and whiskey three times a day; baldness — rub the part morning and evening with onions, till it is red, and afterwards with honey, or, wash with a decoction of boxwood; or electrify it daily."

State Treasurer Ann Richards maintains that holding public office is just like running a household and women do it very well. The proof is in the recipe for biscuits of Nancy Leanorah Matthews — 1840. "The secret to my good biscuits lies in the way I handle my dough. Take one quart of flour, one teaspoon of salt, one teaspoon of soda, large size of hen's egg. If you have any dough left from last cooking, so much the better. I will presume you have." And so forth as you "make a loblolly of it" and bake in quick oven.

Fodder for future Micheners, Fehrenbachs and historians of the state, these recipes provide rare insight into the culture of early Texas. The foredaughters and foremothers were philosophers and scientists. And they had a sense of humor along with a pinch of this and a handful of that. I salute these early Texans. From them, there is much to be learned.

viii

Preface

The Daughters of the Republic of Texas, District VIII, have collected in this book recipes, household hints, and home remedies dating from the days of the Republic to the turn of the century.

One chapter president called a meeting to reminisce with members about family traditions and to compile material that their families still use today. Another chapter uses many of the bread recipes and sells the bread from an historic jailhouse.

Family names appear with the recipe when the material is known to have passed through the family for generations to the present time. Where a year appears with the recipe, the item is known to have been in use at that time. It is our desire for this book to present a concept of a way of life. The pioneer woman maintained many roles — wife, mother, housekeeper, and even doctor at times.

One family ancestor left behind two scrapbooks in which she pasted interesting accounts from news publications of the day. Still another one left her handwritten scrapbook of recipes, household hints, and home remedies. An unusual book used as a source was a handwritten diary from the Civil War era. The Daughters also used handwritten recipes from the Ozona Temperance League.

Some of the original spelling, grammar, and format of the recipes, household hints, and home remedies are retained in this book so that the flavor, customs, and usages of the period would not be lost.

The Daughters of the Republic of Texas, District VIII, is part of a ten-district area of Texas. Members are descended from soldiers and citizens of the Republic of Texas who resided in Texas prior to February 19, 1846. Many of their ancestors fought for the independence of Texas at famous battles such as the Alamo, San Jacinto, and the Siege of Bexar.

Betty Ballinger and Hally Bryan Perry decided in 1891 that the memory of Texas pioneer families and soldiers should forever be perpetuated in the Association of the Daughters of the Republic of Texas. **The Cradle** in Galveston, Texas — a building originally the law office of Miss Ballinger's father — is revered as the place where Miss Ballinger and Miss Perry began their work in 1891.

The French Legation in Austin was constructed in 1840–1841. The historic house was put into the custody of the Daughters by the State of Texas in 1949. The Daughters have restored and maintained the Legation as a museum for the public.

The crusade to save the **Alamo** was launched in 1903 when the sacred ground was about to be sold for a hotel site. Clara Driscoll, leader of the movement to save the Alamo, was a member of

the San Antonio Chapter of the Daughters of the Republic of Texas. She eventually bought the property. In 1905 the state reimbursed her and turned the Alamo over to the care of the Daughters. The Alamo is maintained by the Daughters at no expense to the State of Texas. The DRT Texas History Research Library, located on the Alamo Complex grounds, is maintained by the Daughters for the use of all researchers in Texas history.

A **Texas history museum** is maintained by the Daughters of the Republic of Texas on the second floor of the building which is located on the capitol grounds at Austin. This building was completed in 1857 as a General Land Office. Texas retained her public domain and Land

Department in the annexation treaty with the United States — the only state with such a privilege. In 1916 the Land Department moved, and the vacated building was turned over to the uses and purposes of the Daughters of the Republic of Texas and the Texas Division of the United Daughters of the Confederacy.

Proceeds from this book will be used to encourage historical research into early records of Texas, to foster the preservation of documents and relics, and to encourage the publication of records of the individual service of the soldiers and patriots of the Republic. In addition, funds will be used to secure and memorialize historic areas by erecting markers thereon and to preserve the unity of Texas as achieved and established by the fathers and mothers of the Texas Revolution.

Beverages

COTTAGE BEER
1840

Wheat bran, 1 peck; water, 10 gallons; hops, 3 handfuls; molasses, 2 qts.; yeast, 2 tbsp. Boil the bran and hops in the water until both bran and hops sink to the bottom. Then strain through a hair sieve or thin muslin sheet. When lukewarm, put in the molasses and stir till the molasses is melted. Then put in a cask and add the yeast. When fermentation ceases, bung up. In four days it is ready for use.

OTTAWA BEER
1900

1 oz. each sassafras, allspice, wintergreen, and yellow dock; $1/2$ oz. each wild cherry bark, coriander, and hops; 3 qts. molasses. Pour boiling water on the above; let stand 24 hours. Strain and add $1/2$ pint yeast; let stand 24 hours. Strain and add $1/2$ pint yeast; let stand 24 hours and then bottle.

SPRUCE BEER
1840

1 gallon of water, 1 qt. of good molasses, $1/4$ oz. whole cloves, $1/4$ oz. white ginger root, $1/2$ oz. whole allspice, $1/2$ oz. sassafras. Boil all well — about 3 hours. After taking it off the fire, pour it into a clean tub and add $1^1/2$ gallons of water. Let this stand till milk warm, then add 2 tbsp. of baker's or brewer's yeast; then stand away in the cellar or some cool place during the night, covering it. The next day it will be fit for bottling. One or two raisins, with a few holes punched in them with a fork, placed in each bottle add greatly to its flavor. Pour into strong bottles, cork tightly, and tie down with twine. Set in a cool cellar and in three or four days it will be ripe.

SHAM CHAMPAGNE
1850 — Nancy Leanorah Matthews

The following mixture is warranted to be as noisy as real champagne, and tastes good. Take 1 sliced lemon, 1 spoonful of tartaric acid, 1 oz. of ginger root, and $1^1/2$ lbs. of sugar, and upon them pour 10 qts. of boiling water. When nearly cool, stir in 2 gills of yeast, and then allow the mixture to stand all day in the sun. Cover with a bit of gauze to keep out insects. In the evening, cork and wire it and put it in a cool place. It will be ready for use in 24 hours.

CHOCOLATE
1845

To each quart of new milk, or half milk and water, allow 3 heaping tablespoons of scraped chocolate. It is best to set a coffee pot or any convenient dish into a kettle of boiling water; pour in the milk, and as it heats add the chocolate mixed to a paste with a little milk. Boil for two or three minutes and serve. Some prefer to boil chocolate only 1 minute, others 15, while others boil it 1 hour. Set aside to cool, so that the oil may be removed, and then reheat when wanted.

SPICED CHOCOLATE
1848

Grate 2 squares of chocolate. Boil 1 qt. of milk, reserving a little cold to moisten the chocolate, which must be mixed perfectly smooth to a thin paste. When the milk boils (in which cinnamon must be put when cold, and boiled in it), stir in the chocolate, and let it boil up quickly. Then pour into a pitcher and grate on a little nutmeg. Rich cream added to the milk will improve it.

COCO SYRUP

(Written in back of Grandmother Raven's cookbook; original source or time frame unknown)

$1/2$ cup cocoa   1 cup cold water
$1^1/2$ cups sugar   2 tsp. vanilla
Dash of salt

Mix until dissolved.

COFFEE
1900

"Hunts Breakfast Powder" — Rye roasted with a little butter and ground fine. An excellent substitute for coffee. Boil thoroughly.

Coffee (cheap substitute) — Chop beet root fine, and dry in a closed pan over the fire. Then roast with a little fresh butter until it can be ground.

GINGER ALE
1840 — Nancy Leanorah Matthews

When roots and hops cannot be readily obtained, ginger ale will form an excellent stimulating drink, and it can be made as easily in the city as the country.

Procure 4 oz. of white ginger root and pound or bruise it thoroughly. Mix with it 3 oz. of cream of tartar, then slice up very finely 8 large lemons after squeezing out all the juice. Pour

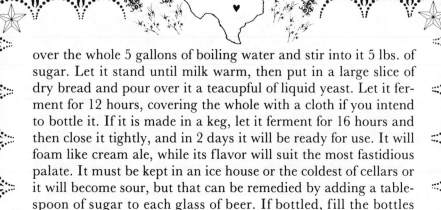

over the whole 5 gallons of boiling water and stir into it 5 lbs. of sugar. Let it stand until milk warm, then put in a large slice of dry bread and pour over it a teacupful of liquid yeast. Let it ferment for 12 hours, covering the whole with a cloth if you intend to bottle it. If it is made in a keg, let it ferment for 16 hours and then close it tightly, and in 2 days it will be ready for use. It will foam like cream ale, while its flavor will suit the most fastidious palate. It must be kept in an ice house or the coldest of cellars or it will become sour, but that can be remedied by adding a tablespoon of sugar to each glass of beer. If bottled, fill the bottles only two-thirds full and fasten the corks with wire or twine.

GRAPE JUICE
(Made from Wild Mustang Grapes)

Gather grapes in July when ripe, pick stems, and wash well. Place in large pot, cover with water, and boil until well done. Strain juice through colander; do not squeeze grapes with hands as the grapes will cause your hands to burn. Pour juice in hot jars and seal.

LEMONADE
1900

To carry in the pocket — Loaf sugar, 1 lb.; rub it down finely in a mortar, and add citric acid, $^1/_2$ oz. (tartaric acid will do), and lemon essence, $^1/_2$ oz., and continue the trituration until all is intimately mixed. (First, it is best to put all the articles into the stove oven when moderately warm, *being separate,* upon paper or plates; let them remain sufficiently long to dry out all dampness absorbed from the air.) Mix and bottle for use. Bottle and cork tight.

A rounding tablespoon can be done up in a paper and carried conveniently in the pocket when persons are going into out-of-the-way places. Added to a half pint of cold water, all the beauties of a lemonade will stand before you waiting to be drank — not costing a penny a glass. This can be made sweeter or more sour, if desired.

TEA
1840

Making tea with cold water — Did anyone ever try making tea with cold water? If you never did, just do so the next warm day when a cool refreshing beverage is desired. Place the tea in a pitcher in the morning, with just enough cold water to cover it. At dinner time fill the pitcher with cold water from the well and you will have the best cup of tea you ever drank — that is for warm weather. The finer qualities of tea are much more fully retained than when steeped upon the fire. And who wishes a cup of scalding tea on coming in straight from the hot harvest field and the scorching glare of our August sun?

CHERRY WINE
1900

Pick and press out the juice of good cherries, White or Black Hearts, or May Dukes, without breaking the stones. (This wine is much improved by adding rasps and red currants; an addition of black currants causes it to resemble port.) To every gallon put 2 lbs. of fine loaf sugar. Put in a cask till the fermentation ceases; stop it closed. In three or four months, bottle it, and in five or six weeks it will be fit to drink.

GRAPE WINE
1840

Ripe, fresh-picked domestic grapes, 20 lbs.; put in a stone jar and pour over them 6 qts. of boiling soft water. When cool enough for the hands, squeeze well, after which let it stand 3 days on the pomace with a cloth thrown over the jar. Then squeeze out the juice; add 10 lbs. of nice crushed sugar. Let it stand a week longer in the jar, then take off the scum. Strain and bottle, leaving a vent until done fermenting; then strain again, bottle tight, and lay the bottles on their sides in a cool place.

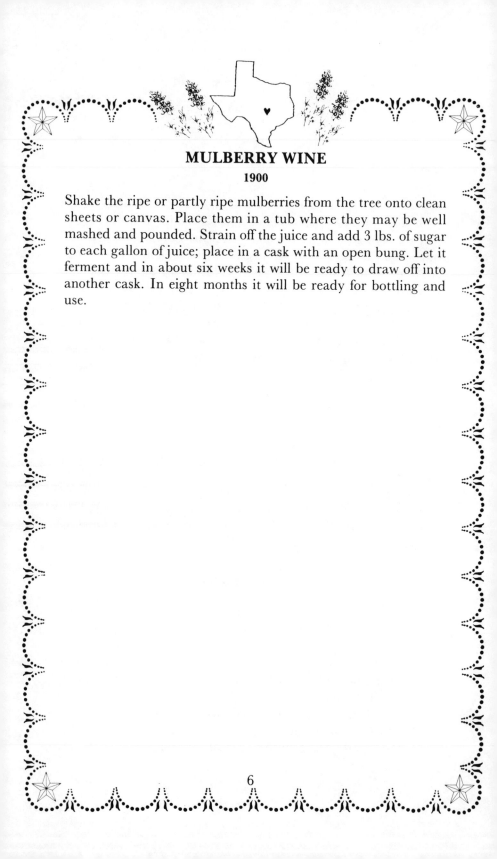

MULBERRY WINE
1900

Shake the ripe or partly ripe mulberries from the tree onto clean sheets or canvas. Place them in a tub where they may be well mashed and pounded. Strain off the juice and add 3 lbs. of sugar to each gallon of juice; place in a cask with an open bung. Let it ferment and in about six weeks it will be ready to draw off into another cask. In eight months it will be ready for bottling and use.

Breads

BISCUITS
1840 — Nancy Leanorah Matthews

The secret to my good biscuits lies in the way I handle my dough. Take 1 qt. of flour, 1 tsp. salt, 1 tsp. soda, lard size of hen's egg. If you have any dough left from last cooking, so much the better. I will presume you have. Sift the flour, soda, and salt into your pan. Then take the old dough, with your lard, and put in the middle of your sifted flour; pour on your sour milk, working the old dough till it gets soft, making a loblolly of it. Then take your flour from the sides of your pan, rub your hands dry, and run under the loblolly. With dry flour, roll it over and over, taking care not to make it stiff. Then roll and cut. The dough should be soft enough to stick to the rolling pin. Bake in a quick oven. It makes the softest, lightest biscuit I have ever seen.

BUTTER ROLLS
1838 — Elizabeth James Standifer

Make biscuit dough. Roll out; cut pieces size of saucer. Sprinkle with cinnamon and sugar and dot with butter. Place in pan until all dough is used. Pour over all with milk. Cook slow.

[Elizabeth came to Texas with her husband and son in 1827 with the Austin Colony. They settled in Bastrop County.]

☆   ☆   ☆

COOKING ADVICE — 1900

"Almost any woman can cook well, if she has plenty with which to do it; but the real science of cooking is to be able to cook a good meal, or dish, with little out of which to make it."

> *"If you attempt the boiling to hurry,*
> *The wood is only wasted;*
> *But, in attempting the baking to hurry,*
> *The food, as well, isn't fit to be tasted."*

☆   ☆   ☆

CORN BREAD: JUST ABOUT
1865 — Salma Dennis King

1 cup cornmeal	a pinch of soda
about 1 tsp. salt	about 1 tsp. baking powder

Mix pretty good. Add 2 beaten eggs. Stir. Add about 1 cup buttermilk, and about 3 tbsp. of oil. Stir a little bit. Cook on top of stove in iron skillet. Cook on one side, then turn.

CORN DODGERS
1853 — Laura Gayle Wilson

(Will keep several days in a saddle bag.) About 2 cups cornmeal, $2/3$ tsp. salt, and enough boiling water so you can pick them up and make a patty (about like a mud patty you made as a child).

These may also be made on a clean shovel at the edge of a campfire. Be sure they are brown on both sides.

These cakes and black coffee made in a tin can on a fire kept many a weary cowboy going on the long trail rides to the railroad.

CORN FRITTERS
1838 — Elizabeth Standifer

1 qt. cornmeal; 1 tbsp. of lard; 2 eggs; 1 tbsp. salt. Scald the meal with the lard in it with boiling water. Cool with a little milk, add the eggs (beaten light); beat very hard for 10 minutes. Make them thin enough with cold milk to drop off the spoon and retain their shape in boiling lard; have the lard boiling hot when you drop them in. Serve hot.

CORNMEAL MUSH
1830 — Nancy Elizabeth Standifer Davis

$1/2$ cup cornmeal, $2^3/4$ cups water, $3/4$ tsp. salt. Sprinkle cornmeal, stirring constantly, into boiling water. Add salt. Cook for $1/2$ hour. Serve with sugar and cream.

CRACKER RECIPE
1850 — Nancy Leanorah Matthews

Mix 1 lb. of fine, white flour; $1/4$ lb. fresh butter; and enough tepid water to work stiff. Beat on the moulding board until soft enough to roll well. Bake in a quick oven. It is brittle, and almost melts in your mouth.

FRIED CAKES
1840

2 eggs, 1 cup of sugar, $1/2$ cup of butter or lard, 1 pt. of sour milk, 1 tsp. of soda, spice, a pinch of salt and flour to roll. Mould hard, roll thin, cut three strips, and braid. Join the ends to form a circle and then fry. Make short strips and fine braids and they will look nice.

FRIED CORN BREAD
1862 — Lillie Bainbridge Connell

1 cup cornmeal	$1/2$ tsp. salt
Lard size of walnut	1 tsp. sugar

Mix ingredients and pour enough boiling water over to make batter. Fry as hot cakes.

Good with greens and buttermilk.

[Lillie Bainbridge Connell moved to Texas from Alabama when a young child. She married Sampson Connell III, who served as sheriff of Williamson County for many years. She was a pioneer woman and it was required that the sheriff and his family reside in living quarters in the county jail. She oversaw the cooking for the prisoners and probably used this recipe.]

GRAHAM BREAD
1870

Fill a large bowl one-third full of water, a little warmer than tepid. Add half a teaspoon of salt and stir in shortening till stiffer than pancake batter. Cover and set where it will keep warm without scalding till light; then turn into a large basin. Add a pint of lukewarm water, half a tablespoon more salt, with two tablespoons of good brown or coffee sugar, and stir in Graham flour till as stiff — not as it can be made, but as it can be conveniently made with a spoon. (If made too stiff the bread will be dry.) Grease the tins; turn in the dough; smooth over the top with a knife or spoon; set again to rise; and when sufficiently light, bake in a tolerably hot oven an hour or more according to the size of the loaves.

HARD TACK BISCUITS
1836 — Asa Wright and John Lloyd Halliburton families

Cut up ¼ lb. butter or lard (½ cup) and mix into 2 lbs. (8 cups) flour. Add 1 salt spoon of salt (1 tsp.) and 3 gills of milk (³/₄ pt.). Knead dough for ½ hour. Cut cakes about as large as a small teacup and ½-inch thick. Prick with a fork and bake in moderate oven until they are a delicate brown.

[This recipe was brought from England; was used on ships at sea; and in Army, Navy, and Confederacy saddlebags. This is a five-generation recipe. Hard tack was made in large supplies and placed in wagons before they left the United States for the Republic of Texas.]

HOE CAKES

1836 — Asa Wright and John Lloyd Halliburton families

To 1 pint yellow cornmeal, add a pinch of salt and pour enough water over the meal to moisten it. Let stand 10 minutes. Then add boiling water until the batter will drop from the spoon. Bake in cakes on a hot griddle greased with salt pork fat. Serve hot with a pat of butter on top of each cake.

[Hoe cakes were called this because they were first made on a hoe over the coals in the fireplace. This was one of the recipes used on the way to the Republic of Texas and for many years later.]

INDIAN CORNMEAL CAKE (Served as a bread)

1830 — Asa Wright and John Lloyd Halliburton families

9 oz. (1½ cups) yellow cornmeal
¼ lb. (½ cup) flour
¾ lb. (1⅔ cups) sugar
½ lb. (1 cup) butter
1 salt spoon (1 tsp.) salt
3 tbsp. rose water (or vanilla)
1 tsp. cinnamon
8 eggs

Mix sugar, butter, eggs; add flour, meal, salt together and mix well. Add to sugar, butter, and egg mixture. Add extract and cinnamon and pour into earthen mold, greased well and powdered with flour. Bake in moderate oven.

[This was first baked in brick oven. Very good and different. Keeps well.]

INDIAN CORN PONE

Mix four cups cornmeal and 1 tsp. salt. Pour 1½ cups boiling water onto dry ingredients and mix well; cool and then form into patties. Fry in hot lard until brown. Pour molasses or honey over them and enjoy.

MOLASSES BREAD
1895 — Grandmother Horn

Take around 1 cup molasses and a cup or so of sugar. Mix with 1 cup butter and 1 cup buttermilk. Add 3 eggs and mix well. Then add 1 tsp. each of saleratus (baking soda) and ginger. Put in about 1 tsp. cloves and a teaspoon or so of cinnamon. Put in a dash of salt. Stir in 5 or so cups of white flour; sift it first. Stir well. Bake in hot oven.

[Tastes like moist gingerbread. Good with preserves or butter.]

OATCAKES

Mix two cups oatmeal with a pinch of salt and a pinch of soda. Make a well in the center. Add 3 tbsp. melted lard with 3 tbsp. warm water mixed with 3 tbsp. milk. Mix together to form a soft dough. Knead lightly on board sprinkled with oatmeal and roll out thinly into two rounds. Cut into quarters, place on greased baking sheet and toast in moderate oven for 30 minutes till slightly brown and crisp.

[The original recipe for oatcakes was simply oatmeal in cold water. One side was cooked on a griddle or flatstone over very hot coals. The other side was toasted in front of the coals. Different oatcakes were baked for different occasions — the first day of every season, when a child was born or cutting its first tooth. Whatever the occasion, they are good for breakfast with plenty of butter and jelly, honey, or preserves.]

OLD SPOON BREAD
1836 — Asa Wright and John Lloyd Halliburton families

Mix 1 cup cornmeal, 2 cups cold water, and 1½ tsp. salt. Boil for 5 minutes. Stir constantly. Remove from stove and add 1 cup milk and 2 tbsp. melted fat and mix well. Add 3 well-beaten eggs and 1 level tsp. baking powder. Beat well. Pour into well-greased pan or skillet and bake in a slow oven for an hour and fifteen minutes. Serve hot from the pan in which it was baked.

[You will have to try this to believe how delicious it is.]

PLAIN WHITE FAMILY BREAD

Take one pint of flour and half a pint of good hop yeast and stir it together about five o'clock in the afternoon; at nine put one-half gallon of flour in a tray; put the sponge in the middle of the flour with a piece of lard as large as a walnut. Knead it all up with tepid water made salty with two teaspoonfuls or more to taste; work it well, and put it in a jar to rise. Next morning knead it over with a little flour; make it in two loaves; and set it in a warm place or oven until ready. Then put it to bake. When done, wrap it in a nice coarse towel. If you have no sugar in the yeast you use, stir a large teaspoonful in it before putting it in the flour.

PONE
1891

This is a dish prepared by the Indians, called also *paune*. Take two cupfuls of cornmeal, two of wheat flour, one of sugar, and half a cup of melted butter. Add one egg, one teaspoonful of salt, one of soda, and two of cream of tartar. Mix with enough milk to make a moderately stiff batter, and bake in a hot oven.

PONTUCK
1830 — Rebecca Caroline Burnett Lee

There is a root that grows in Harris County, out of which the Bedias (Indians) made a kind of bread, which even in their rude making was palatable. We once took dinner with Francisco and this bread, known as pontuck, was served at dinner. The way this bread was made, a squaw would chip up the root with a hatchet. Two holes were dug in a moist place, one a little higher than the other, and a bunch of moss placed between them. The chipped particles were placed in the higher hole. The woman would work them up, throw off the coarser particles, and allow the finer to filter through the moss, settling into the lower place. Later it was dipped up to be cooked. This wild root, if treated under scientific processes, would probably furnish the most delicious kind of bread.

13

POTATO BISCUITS
1840

Boil mealy potatoes; pare and mash them. Put two good-sized ones to a quart of Graham flour, and rub them in as you would shortening. Then wet with sweet milk or water, knead well, roll, cut into small biscuits, prick with a fork, and bake in a quick oven.

PRONTO RANCH BISCUITS
1860 — Grandma Garner

Sift 2 cups white flour with around 4 tsp. baking powder and a little salt. (Grandma usually meant about $1/2$ tsp. when she said "little.") Cut in about 4 tbsp. or so of lard. Good clear bacon fat is best. Add $3/4$ cup fresh milk, mixing well and get a fairly stiff dough. Take a greased pan and drop the dough by spoonfuls. "A good hot woodstove oven should be used" to cook till brown.

RICE BREAD
1891

After a pint of rice has been boiled soft, mix it with two quarts of rice flour or wheat flour. When cold, add half a teaspoonful of yeast, a teaspoonful of salt, and enough milk to make a soft dough. When it has risen, bake in small buttered pans.

RYE BREAD
1890

Scald two handfuls of cornmeal with a quart of boiling water and add a quart of milk and a tablespoon of salt. When cool, add a teacupful of yeast, and enough rye flour to make it as stiff as wheat-bread dough. After it has risen, put it in pans and bake an hour and a half.

SHORTNIN' BREAD

Mix together 2 cups flour, $1/2$ tsp. cinnamon, and $1/4$ tsp. nutmeg in large bowl. Dissolve $1 1/2$ tsp. baking soda in $1/2$ cup of buttermilk. Mix $1/3$ cup of butter with 1 cup molasses; bring to a boil

while stirring. Add to flour mixture; stir in buttermilk and 1 beaten egg. Pour into greased and floured cast-iron skillet and bake for 30 minutes or until done. Cool in skillet.

SPIDER CORN CAKE
Ruthie Isabelle Pullin Maley

Beat 2 eggs and $\frac{1}{4}$ cup of sugar together. Add 1 cup sweet milk and 1 cup sour milk, to which has been added 1 tsp. soda. Add 1 tsp. salt. Mix $1\frac{2}{3}$ cups granulated cornmeal and $\frac{1}{3}$ cup flour.

Put a spider skillet on the range and when it is hot, melt in 2 tbsp. of butter. Turn the spider so that the butter will coat the bottom and sides. Pour in the corn cake mixture, then carefully pour over one more cup of sweet milk. Do not stir. Bake in a moderate oven 20 to 35 minutes. It will have a streak of custard through the cake. Serve with molasses or a sprinkle of brown sugar.

Texas pioneer cooks made many corn recipes to be used either as a custard or as bread.

[Ruthie Isabelle Pullin Maley descended from the Mississippi Pullins and Nelsons and was a wonderfully resourceful cook for a large farm family!]

STUFFING FOR POULTRY OR PORK
1900 — Mrs. Bertie Hancock Smith

Break 1 pan of corn bread in a large mixing bowl; add one-half loaf of white yeast bread and add 6 or 8 biscuits. Moisten with a quart of chicken broth. To that mixture add 4 beaten eggs, 4 minced onions fried in butter, 2 cups of chopped celery, $\frac{1}{4}$ cup of raisins, 2 tbsp. of sage, and a dash of salt and pepper. Mix and fold in 1 cup of cooked rice to the mixture. Stuff the bird and cook the remaining dressing in baking dish until light brown.

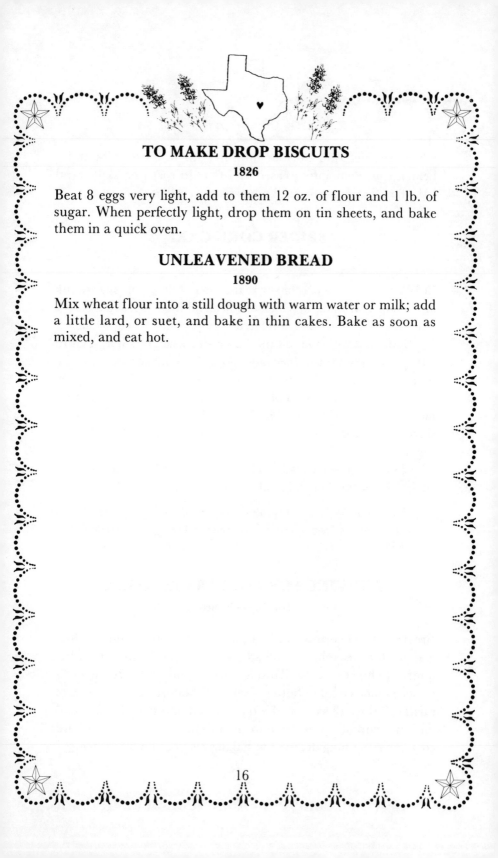

TO MAKE DROP BISCUITS
1826

Beat 8 eggs very light, add to them 12 oz. of flour and 1 lb. of sugar. When perfectly light, drop them on tin sheets, and bake them in a quick oven.

UNLEAVENED BREAD
1890

Mix wheat flour into a still dough with warm water or milk; add a little lard, or suet, and bake in thin cakes. Bake as soon as mixed, and eat hot.

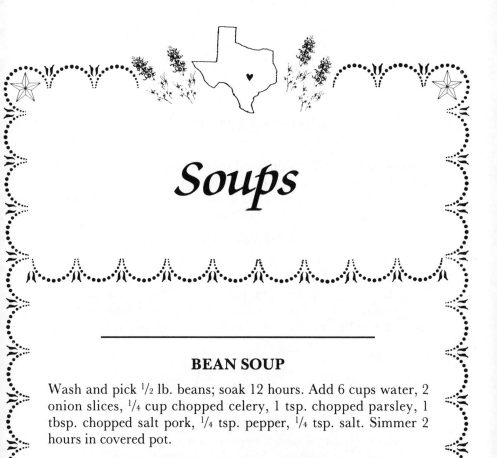

Soups

BEAN SOUP

Wash and pick ¹/₂ lb. beans; soak 12 hours. Add 6 cups water, 2 onion slices, ¹/₄ cup chopped celery, 1 tsp. chopped parsley, 1 tbsp. chopped salt pork, ¹/₄ tsp. pepper, ¹/₄ tsp. salt. Simmer 2 hours in covered pot.

BIERSUPPE (BEER SOUP)

Scald 2 cups milk; do not boil. Mix 2 tsp. cornstarch and ¹/₂ cup sugar and add 3 egg yolks. Blend thoroughly before stirring slowly into the milk. In a separate pan scald the beer. Combine with the milk mixture. Add 1 tbsp. sugar to the 3 beaten egg whites and heap by tablespoon on top of soup.

BREAD SOUP
1890 — Grandma Martha Koehler

Scald 2 cups of sweet milk. In a frying pan brown 1 cup torn bread crusts in butter till well coated and brown. Pour milk in soup bowl and top with the bread. A pinch of sugar may be added if desired.

[This was usually served when someone wasn't feeling well.]

17

BROWN RABBIT SOUP
1840

Disjoint rabbit, roll in flour, and fry in brown butter. Put this in kettle and cover with 3 quarts of boiling water. Season with salt, pepper, and 1 minced onion. Boil 3 hours. Thicken with brown flour and send to the table with fried bread crusts.

CHEESE SOUP

Put ¼ cup butter in heavy skillet. Fry vegetables of ½ cup each onions, carrots, and celery till tender. Stir in ¼ cup flour and 1½ tbsp. cornstarch. Cook till bubbly. Add 4 cups chicken stock and 4 cups milk slowly, blending into a smooth sauce. Add ⅛ tsp. soda, 1 lb. cubed cheese, and 1 tsp. salt. Stir till cheese is melted.

CORN SOUP
1880

½ lb. of salt pork diced and browned in hot spider with 1 onion, 1 qt. water, 1 bowl of diced potatoes, 2 cups corn, 1 tbsp. butter (browned), 1 tbsp. flour, 2 cups of milk. Cook corn, potatoes, onion, and meat until done, then add browned butter, milk, and the flour just before serving.

GREEN PEA SOUP

Boil the empty pods of a half-peck of green peas in 1 gallon of water for 1 hour; strain them out. Add 4 pounds of beef cut into small pieces, and boil slowly for an hour and a half longer. Half an hour before serving, add the shelled peas, and 20 minutes later half a cup of rice flour, salt, pepper, and a little chopped parsley. After adding the rice flour, stir frequently so as to prevent scorching.

MARROW DUMPLING SOUP
1800 — Annabelle Koehler Augusta Below

Remove the marrow from a beef-leg soup bone. Put the bone and meat on to boil in 3 qts. cold water with a large onion chopped fine. Bring to a boil slowly and cook several hours; ½ hour before serving time, strain. Put back over fire and season with salt and pepper. When briskly boiling put in dumplings made as follows: Grate 4 large slices of stale bread; add the marrow, 2 eggs, a little nutmeg, salt and pepper, 1 tbsp. flour, and make into little dumplings the size of a hickory nut. Drop into the boiling soup. Boil 15 minutes, then serve.

OATMEAL PORRIDGE
1840 — From Grandmother Matthews's Scrapbook

Oatmeal porridge is made with milk and water, in proportion of one part of the former to two of latter. Allow two ounces of oatmeal to a pint and a half of milk and water, and boil half an hour.

OKRA SOUP

Take a nice joint of beef filled with marrow, 1 gallon water, 1 onion cut fine, 2 sprigs parsley, half a peck of okra, and 1 qt. tomatoes. Boil meat six hours, add vegetables, and boil two more hours.

ONION SOUP
1890

Slice 10 medium-sized onions and fry brown in butter with 1 1/2 tbsp. flour. Put into a saucepan, and stir in slowly four or five pints of milk and water (about one-third water). Season to taste and add a teacupful of grated potato. Set in a kettle of boiling water, and cook ten minutes; add a cup of sweet cream and serve quickly.

OX-TAIL SOUP
1890

Chop the ox-tail into small pieces. Set on the fire with a tablespoonful of butter, stir until brown, and then pour off the fat. Add broth to taste, and boil gently until the pieces of tail are well

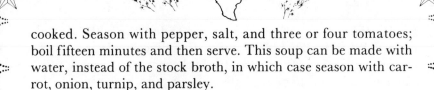

cooked. Season with pepper, salt, and three or four tomatoes; boil fifteen minutes and then serve. This soup can be made with water, instead of the stock broth, in which case season with carrot, onion, turnip, and parsley.

OYSTER SOUP
1900

To each dozen or dish of oysters put $1/2$ pint of water; milk, 1 gill; butter, $1/2$ oz.; powdered crackers to thicken. Bring the oysters and water to a boil, then add the other ingredients previously mixed together, and boil from 3 to 5 minutes only. Each one will choose to add salt, pepper, etc., to their own taste.

POTATO SOUP

Slice 4 potatoes and 1 onion. Add about a cup of dried beef cut in small pieces. Cook until tender in 3 pts. of water; season with plenty of butter, pepper, and salt. Add 1 pt. of milk, with 2 tsp. flour stirred in it.

ROSE HIP SOUP

Soak 4 oz. dried rose hips and boil in 1 pt. of water with lemon rind, 1 cinnamon stick, and 3 cloves until they are soft. Rub through a fine sieve. Brown 1 oz. flour in 1 oz. fat and gradually add the soup. Sweeten to taste. Gradually add 1 tbsp. white wine.

SQUIRREL STEW
1818 — Elizabeth Denton English

Clean and skin squirrel. Cut in serving size pieces. Place pieces in Dutch oven or heavy skillet with lid. Cover with water and steam until the meat is nearly tender. Add 4 ribs of celery, small whole onions, small whole potatoes, 4 carrots (sliced diagonally), 1 small bay leaf, and salt and pepper. Cook until tender.

If thickened gravy is desired, add 1 tbsp. of flour dissolved in $1/2$ cup of water. This is good with cornbread.

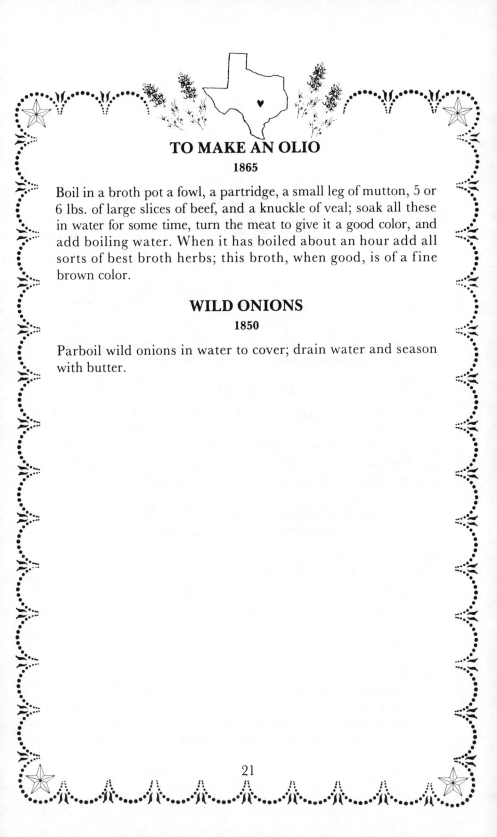

TO MAKE AN OLIO
1865

Boil in a broth pot a fowl, a partridge, a small leg of mutton, 5 or
6 lbs. of large slices of beef, and a knuckle of veal; soak all these
in water for some time, turn the meat to give it a good color, and
add boiling water. When it has boiled about an hour add all
sorts of best broth herbs; this broth, when good, is of a fine
brown color.

WILD ONIONS
1850

Parboil wild onions in water to cover; drain water and season
with butter.

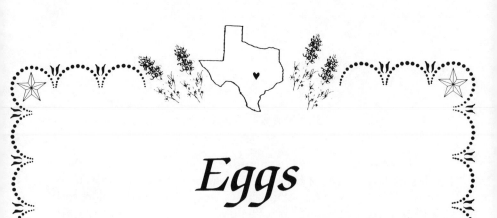

Eggs

EGG BALLS

Yolks of 2 hard-boiled eggs   **Few grains cayenne**
¹/₄ tsp. salt   **¹/₂ tsp. melted butter**

Rub eggs through sieve, add seasonings, moisten with raw egg yolk to make of consistency to handle. Shape in small balls, roll in flour, and sauté in butter. Serve with clear soup.

COLORED (EASTER) EGGS

1840 — Nancy Leanorah Matthews

Whether for Easter, or ornamental purposes, it is a nice thing for young people to know how to color eggs. Here is a good recipe. To color eggs a fine, bright red, get five cents' worth of cochineal from the druggist. Into boiling water put a part of it, dissolved in a little water. Put in all the eggs you wish to color red, boil a few moments, remove part of the eggs, then add half of the remaining cochineal. Boil a few minutes longer, then remove more of the eggs. Throw in the rest of the coloring; boil and you have the rest of the eggs a deep shade of red. You have three shades of red, and can have more by adding the color gradually. Several shades of yellow can be made by using a little gamboge, to be had also of the druggist. Coffee will make the eggs a beautiful brown.

Onion skins will make still another color; and bright colored cotton prints, tied round the eggs before boiling, will mark them very prettily. The water should boil very hard to extract the color from the cloth. After the eggs are boiled in some bright color they may be ornamented in a great variety of ways by using a sharp pen-knife and etching monograms, landscapes, faces or flowers, birds or insects upon them. These make very unique and attractive little tokens of remembrance for friends — especially as they are supposed to be very hard-boiled and will never decompose.

FRIED HAM AND EGG (A Breakfast Dish)
1870

Cut the ham into slices, and take care that they are of the same thickness in every part. Cut off the rind, and if the ham should be particularly hard and salty it will be found an improvement to soak it for about 10 minutes in hot water, and then dry it in a cloth. Put it into a cold frying pan, set it over the fire, and turn the slices 3 or 4 times whilst they are cooking. When done, place them on a dish, which should be kept hot in front of the fire during the time the eggs are being poached. Poach the eggs; slip them on the slices of ham, and serve.

HOW TO CHOOSE EGGS

In putting the hand round the egg, and presenting to the light, the end which is not covered, it should be transparent. If you can detect some tiny spots, it is not newly laid, but may be very good for all ordinary purposes except boiling soft. If you see a large spot near the shell, it is bad, and should not be used on any account. The white of a newly-laid egg boiled soft is like milk; that of an egg a day old is like rice boiled in milk; and that of an old egg, compact, tough, and difficult to digest. A cook ought not to give eggs two or three days old to people who really care for fresh eggs, under the delusion that they will not find any difference; for an amateur will find it out in a moment, not only by the appearance, but also by the taste.

23

Keep hens quiet and well fed if you wish to fatten them but make them scratch for their living if you desire eggs.

☆　　☆　　☆

HOW TO KEEP EGGS FRESH
1840

All it is necessary to do to keep eggs through summer is to procure small, clean wooden or tin vessels, holding from 10 to 20 gallons, and a barrel, more or less, or common, fine-ground land plaster. Begin by putting on the bottom of the vessel 2 or 3 inches of plaster. Then, having fresh eggs, with the yolks unbroken, set them up, small end down, close to each other but not crowding, and make the first layer. Then add more plaster and enough so the eggs will stand upright, and set up the second layer; then another deposit of plaster, followed by a layer of eggs, till the vessel is full. Finish by covering the top layer with plaster. Eggs so packed and subjected to a temperature of at least 85 degrees, if not 90 degrees, during August and September, came out fresh, and if one could be certain of not having a temperature of more than 75 degrees to contend with, I am confident eggs could be kept by these means all the year round. Observe that the eggs must be fresh laid, the yolks unbroken, the packing done in small vessels, and with clean, fine-ground land plaster, and care must be taken that no egg so presses on another as to break the shell.

Eggs may be kept good for a year in the following manner:

To a pail of water, put of unslacked lime and coarse salt each a pint; keep it in a cellar, or cool place, and put the eggs in, as fresh laid as possible. It is well to keep a stone pot of this lime water ready to receive the eggs as soon as laid. Make a fresh supply every few months. This lime water is of exactly the proper strength; strong lime water will cook the eggs. Very strong lime water will eat the shell.

OYSTER OMELET
1876 — Margaret Emma Davis

Chop fine 12 large oysters, beat 6 eggs, and add a spoonful of flour, rubbed smooth in milk. Season with salt, pepper, and a little melted butter; fry in one omelet and serve hot.

☆   ☆   ☆

PREPARING BREAKFAST — 1850

Always get your material for breakfast ready overnight; fix the fire all ready to light, fill the tea-kettle, grind the coffee, and prepare the potatoes, and thus you can sleep half an hour longer in the morning.

☆   ☆   ☆

SOUR EGGS (German Style)

Stir 1 tbsp. of flour into 1 tbsp. of butter in a hot pan until well browned. Take ½ teacup vinegar filled up with water. Salt and pepper to taste. Pour into the browned flour and let boil up. Break the eggs in one at a time until the pan is full. Baste the top with the gravy until the eggs are cooked hard or soft according to taste.

TO MAKE AN OMELET
1849 — Jeanette Dyer Davis

Break 6 or 8 eggs in a dish; beat them a little. Add parsley and chives chopped small, with pepper and salt. Mix all well together, put a piece of butter in a pan, let it melt over a clear fire till nearly brown; pour in the eggs, stir it in, and in a few minutes it will be done sufficiently. Double it and dish it quite hot.

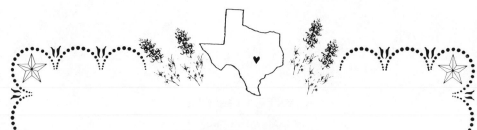

Fish

BAKED SHAD
1890

Many people are of the opinion that the very best method of cooking a shad is to bake it. Stuff it with bread crumbs, salt, pepper, butter, and parsley, and mix this up with beaten yolk of egg; fill the fish with it, and sew it up or fasten a string around it. Pour over it a little water and some butter, and bake as you would a fowl. A shad will require from an hour to an hour and a quarter to bake.

CODDLED OYSTERS
1900

6 or 8 oysters to each person	2 sprigs of parsley, chopped
6 slices of bread	very fine
1 large tbsp. of butter	1 bay leaf, minced fine
1/2 tsp. salt	3 cloves
1/2 tsp. black pepper	1 blade of mace
Dash of cayenne	1 pint of oyster liquor

Toast five or six slices of bread to a nice brown and butter them on both sides. Drain the liquor from the oysters and put it in a saucepan. When hot, add a large lump of butter. Have ready a

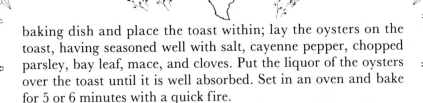

baking dish and place the toast within; lay the oysters on the toast, having seasoned well with salt, cayenne pepper, chopped parsley, bay leaf, mace, and cloves. Put the liquor of the oysters over the toast until it is well absorbed. Set in an oven and bake for 5 or 6 minutes with a quick fire.

CRAWFISH
1900

Put live crawfish in boiling salted water with caraway seed (2 qts. water, 1 tbsp. salt, and 1 tbsp. caraway). Boil 5 minutes; let stand until cool. Drain and serve.

FROG LEGS
1900

Boil the frog legs in salt water and drain. Heat 2 tbsp. butter; add 1/2 cup soup stock, 1/2 cup Madeira wine, salt and cayenne pepper to taste. Boil 3 minutes. Add 1/2 pt. cream and 3 yolks slightly beaten. Cook 2 minutes, stirring constantly, and pour over frog legs.

LOBSTER PIE

2 lobsters	Mace, salt, pepper
Nutmeg	1 egg yolk
Pepper, Salt	2 tbsp. butter
Make in force-meat balls:	Pie Crust:
1/2 cup bread crumbs	2 hard-cooked eggs
1 tsp. parsley	1 cup white sauce
1 anchovy, mashed	1/2 cup white wine
1 tsp. lemon peel, grated	1 tbsp. lemon juice

Boil lobster; cool, and remove meat. Season with salt, pepper, and nutmeg and put in pie pan on top of bottom pie crust. Make bread crumbs and seasoning into force-meat balls and put on top of lobster. Add hard-cooked eggs, 1 cup of white sauce, wine, lemon juice. Then cover with pie crust and bake until crust is browned.

OYSTERS AND BACON
1900

3 dozen oysters	Thin slices of breakfast bacon
Minced parsley	Sauce piquante

Wrap each oyster in a very thin slice of breakfast bacon. Lay on a broiler over a baking pan in a hot oven. Remove when the bacon is brown. Each must be fastened with a wooden toothpick. Serve with minced parsley and pepper sauce, or sauce piquante.

SAUCE PIQUANTE

2 onions	2 pickles, 2 inches in length
1 tbsp. butter	1 tsp. strong French vinegar
2 cloves of garlic	Salt and pepper to taste
1 sprig each of thyme, parsley, and bay leaf	Cayenne or hot pepper

Chop 2 onions very fine. Smother in a tablespoonful of butter. When well cooked, without burning, add a tablespoonful of consomme or water. Add 2 cloves of garlic, minced very fine, and the herbs minced very fine. Season to taste with hot pepper. Take two pickles and cut into thin slices of about a quarter of an inch in thickness. Put this into the sauce, with a teaspoonful of strong vinegar, and let the whole boil about five minutes. Serve with boiled beef, boiled beef tongue, boiled pork tongue, or any boiled meats.

PEPPERS STUFFED WITH FISH

Scoop out seeds of peppers and parboil 15 minutes. Fill with mixture of leftover fish broken in small pieces, salt, pepper, cheese, and cream sauce. Put bread crumbs on top of each pepper and dot with butter. Bake in oven until brown and peppers are done. Serve with catsup.

SCALING A FISH

Hold it by the tail under water (which is salted) in a deep pan, and with a small, sharp knife held slanting, scrape the scales from the tail to head. The scales will come off easier under water and will fall to the bottom of the pan instead of flying about.

☆   ☆   ☆

TO DRESS CRABS
1811

Take out the meat and clean it from the skin. Put it into a pan with half a pint of white wine, a little nutmeg, pepper, and salt. Over a slow fire, throw in a few crumbs of bread, beat up one yolk of an egg with one spoonful of vinegar, then shake the pan round a minute, and serve.

TO FRY OYSTERS

Dry your oysters well, either in a colander or by spreading on a clean, dry cloth. Take fine cornmeal and season well with salt and pepper. Roll the oysters in the meal and fry at once in boiling lard while the meal is still dry. Cook to a light brown.

[George Maley, citizen and soldier of the Republic of Texas, dearly loved all seafood. Almost every year found the Maley family camped on the Texas coast at Copano Bay. Their black iron skillet was often used to fry oysters. But Grandpa George liked best to wade out to the oyster reef and, aided by his trusty knife, open the shell and pop the oyster into his mouth!]

TO PITCH EELS
1826 — Sarah Stafford Dyer

Skin and wash your eels, then dry them with a cloth. Sprinkle them with pepper, salt, and a little dried sage. Turn them backward and forward, and skewer them; rub a gridiron with beef

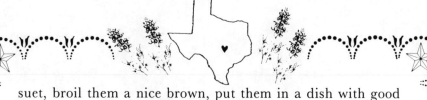

suet, broil them a nice brown, put them in a dish with good melted butter, and lay around fried parsley.

[Sarah S. Dyer was born in Virginia and came to Texas with Stephen F. Austin, her father, and stepmother when fourteen years old.]

WHITE FISH
1890

This fish may be broiled, fried, or baked. To bake it, prepare a stuffing of fine bread crumbs, with a little salt pork chopped very fine. Season with sage, parsley, pepper, and salt. Fill the fish with the stuffing, sew it up, sprinkle the outside with salt, pepper, and flour, and bake. In frying white fish, pour off the fat as it accumulates, as it is apt to be too fat when served.

Meat

BAKED HAM
1840

Make a thick paste of flour and water (not boiled) and cover the entire ham with it, bone and all; put in a pan on a spider or two muffin rings, or anything that will keep it an inch from the bottom, and bake in a hot oven; if a small ham, 15 minutes. The oven should be hot when put in and the paste forms a hard crust round the ham, and the skin comes off with it.

BAKED POSSUM
1840

Salt and pepper inside of 1 skinned and gutted possum. Place in a roasting pan with a small amount of water in bottom. Bake for an hour in slow oven. Remove lid and continue to bake until skin is brown.

☆   ☆   ☆

A TIP ON TOUGH MEAT — 1900

In cooking tough fowl or meat, 1 tbsp. of vinegar in the water will save nearly 2 hours' boiling.

☆   ☆   ☆

31

BAKED RACCOON
1840

Boil 1 skinned and gutted coon in water for an hour to tenderize. Remove, dry, and rub skin with butter. Place 1 tart apple and 2 medium onions inside of coon. Season with salt and pepper. Place coon in roasting pan with a little water in bottom. Cover with fat meat. Bake in moderate oven until tender.

☆　　☆　　☆

BEE STINGS

Nothing is more effectual than lean raw meat. It is said to also cure the bite of a rattlesnake.

☆　　☆　　☆

BREAST OF VEAL, GLACÉE
1865

Cut your breast as square as possible; bone it and draw the cut pieces together with a thread. Put it into a pan with a ladle of veal bouillon, cover it with slices of salt pork, and a buttered paper, previously adding 2 carrots in bits, 4 onions in slices, 2 bay leaves, 2 cloves, pepper and salt. Put some coals on the lid as well as below. When two-thirds done take out the vegetables, reduce your gravy to jelly, turn your meat, and set on the cover till done. It takes in all two hours and a half over a gentle fire.

BRISKET OF BEEF

Put the part with the hard fat into a stewpot, with a small quantity of water. Let it boil up, and skim it thoroughly; then add carrots, turnips, onions, celery, and a few peppercorns. Stew till extremely tender; then take out the flat bones and remove all the fat from the soup. Serve that and the meat in a tureen, or the soup alone, and the meat on a dish garnished with some vegetables. The following sauce is much admired, served with the beef: Take a half pint of the soup and mix it with a spoonful of catsup,

a glass of port wine, teaspoonful of made mustard, a little flour, a bit of butter, and salt. Boil all together a few minutes, then pour it around the meat.

BROILED HAM WITH CUCUMBER GARNISH
1900

Cut thin as many slices of ham as desired and broil evenly over hot coals. Then well brown butter, add pepper, and serve with slices of cucumber that have been steeped in salted vinegar several hours arranged around it.

CALVES HEADCHEESE
1850

Boil calves head till meat leaves the bones. Pick it free of bone. Season with 1 tbsp. of salt and 1 tsp. of pepper and 1 tbsp. of any sweet herbs that you may like. Pack closely in a dish and put a small plate over it, with a weight upon it. When cold and firm, slice for tea or sandwiches. Mustard is nice with it.

CHICKEN AND RICE
1835 — Agnes Coreth Meusebach

1 young chicken cut up ($2\frac{1}{2}$ or 3 lbs.); salt, butter or other cooking oil; 1 cup of dry white rice (do not wash); teakettle of boiling water. In a deep pot with lid, place shortening and brown chicken on both sides. Remove; pour dry rice in hot shortening and stir until brown. Place chicken pieces on top of browned rice and shortening; cover with boiling water. Place lid on pot, turn heat low, and let water absorb into rice (can add broth). Will be tender when absorbed. Serve with tender green asparagus, green beans, carrots, or beets.

CHICKEN PIE
1840

An old chicken will do for this purpose. Singe and draw the fowl, cutting it up in joints. Cover with cold water and let it simmer, closely covered, for an hour or more, according to its age. Then add 3 medium-sized onions, sliced, some sprigs of parsley, salt and pepper, and continue cooking until the meat is tender and the onions done. Dish the bulky pieces, such as the back, under part of the breast and first joints.

Make a batter with an egg, a cup of milk, and a teaspoonful of baking powder sifted through enough flour to make it of cupcake consistency. Drop this into the boiling broth in small spoonfuls.

While the dumplings are cooking, which will take about 8 minutes, heat to boiling half a pint of milk; pour this into the gravy after the rest of the meat and the dumplings have been removed, and stir in a lump of butter and a large tablespoonful of flour wet with a little cold milk. Boil for a minute and pour over the chicken. The dumplings should be served on a separate dish. Bake a piece of rich piecrust the size of a dinner plate; break into as many pieces as there are people to be served, and place as a border around the dish containing the meat. This is chicken *par excellence,* and if your family is large you need not be afraid to prepare two chickens. If any is left, heat for breakfast: add a little soup stock, or thickened hot milk if more gravy is necessary, and pour the whole over some slices of buttered toast. If the fowl is old and fat, it would be advisable to remove as much as possible of the fat and skin before cooking.

COUNTRY SMOTHERED CHICKEN
1836 — Asa Wright

Cut one large broiler, about 3 lbs., in serving pieces. Salt and coat with flour. Put about $1/2$ cup lard in an iron skillet. When hot, add chicken and brown on both sides. Cover completely with hot water. Season to taste with salt and pepper and bake till tender.

> [*This recipe was for a woodstove. Modern ovens evaporate the milk more, so cover with foil while baking in moderate oven. A fat hen may take the place of a fryer or a broiler.*]

CREOLE CHICKEN
1894 — Irene Odom Linscomb

2 frying sized chickens	1 tbsp. lard
2 green peppers, chopped fine	1 tbsp. butter
2 onions, chopped fine	4 tomatoes, stewed

Fry chicken until brown in lard and butter, and then fry onions and green peppers about 5 or 10 minutes. Mix onions, tomatoes, green pepper, and lemon together and simmer slowly 30 to 40 minutes, together with the chicken added. Add salt and a little red pepper. Serve with rice.

CURING AND PACKING PORK
1840 — Nancy Leanorah Matthews

Hams and shoulders are cured thus: A mixture of one-fourth brown sugar and three-fourths dry salt is made. Place the hams and shoulders in a large salting tub, skin side downward, and then cover with the above mixture, say $1/3$ of an inch thick, a little salt and sugar being applied from time to time on such parts of the meat as become uncovered by the formation of brine, taking care to keep them well covered near the bone. Shoulders and hams from hogs weighing 300 pounds are required to be kept in a tub under this treatment about three weeks. They are then hung up in a dry room for a week, and afterwards hung up in a smokehouse and smoked about a month. They should then be sewed in cotton bags and lime washed. Corn cobs are the best for smoking.

DRIED VENISON

Cut venison in 2-inch slices, any length; place in a brine made with cold water and enough salt to float an egg. Let set 12 to 18 hours. Remove from brine and string on string. Dip in hot water until color of meat turns whitish. Sprinkle with coarse black pepper. Hang up and smoke for 2 or 3 days. Will be ready to eat in about a week.

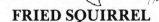

FRIED SQUIRREL

1818 — Elizabeth Denton English

Rinse skinned squirrel in cold water and pat dry. Dip in buttermilk and then in seasoned flour and fry in hot fat. If the squirrel is young, steaming is not necessary. Otherwise, drain off excess fat, add 1 cup water, and steam covered. Make gravy in the frying pan by adding the leftover seasoned flour and milk or water. Serve with hot biscuits and wild plum jelly.

GAME PIE

12 doves or other small birds	12 hard-boiled eggs
pie crust	2 cups egg dressing
salt and pepper	

Stuff birds with egg dressing. Put them in a stew pan with water to cover. Let them cook until nearly tender. Season with salt and pepper and 2 tbsp. butter. Thicken gravy with 1 tbsp. flour, let cook 10 minutes more. Remove to cool. Butter a deep dish and line with pie crust. Have ready the eggs cut in slices. Put a layer of eggs and a layer of birds until dish is full. Pour gravy over all and cover with rest of crust. Bake till light brown.

Egg dressing:

4 hard-boiled eggs, chopped	¹/₂ tsp. sage
	1 chopped onion
1 cup bread, wet and squeezed	1 tsp. butter
	salt and pepper to taste

Fry onion in butter; add bread and other ingredients already mixed in. Fry 10 minutes; add seasoning. Stuff birds.

GUMBO FILE

Elizabeth Barrow Barber

Many of the French-influenced portions of Texas still use sassafras powder in their gumbo recipes. Add it just after the gumbo is cooked and before serving. It thickens the gumbo. The Choc-

taw Indians prepared the herb by drying the leaves and pounding them into a powder on a stone mortar. This powder is called Gumbo File.

CREOLE GUMBO: CHICKEN AND OYSTERS
Elizabeth Barrow Barber

Cut a 2-lb. chicken into serving pieces. Sprinkle with salt and pepper and dredge with flour. In a large, heavy kettle or skillet with close-fitting lid, melt 4 tbsp. butter, ¼ lb. of diced salt pork. Bring all to frying point and drop in the chicken pieces. Fry for about 20 minutes, turning often to brown on all sides. Add ½ cup chopped onion, 1 bay leaf, ½ tsp. thyme, ¼ tsp. cayenne pepper. Stir to mix well. Add 1 qt. oyster stock and 2 cups boiling water. Cover and cook slowly until chicken is very tender. When ready to serve add Gumbo File and 2 dozen oysters. Serve over hot rice.

[Elizabeth Barrow Barber was a citizen of the Republic of Texas.]

HOGSHEAD CHEESE
1874

Use 1 small pig's head, or half a large head, and 4 pig feet (have cleaned and trimmed at the market). These make the cheese firmer, and less fat. Put in a kettle with water enough to cover; boil slowly until all the bones will slip out. Then set away. When cold, skim all the fat off the top. Then set the kettle back on the stove until it warms the meat. Set off, skim out the meat into a chopping bowl, and work through the hands to remove all the small bones. Season highly with pepper, salt, powdered thyme, summer savory, allspice, and cinnamon. Chop fine and add some of the liquor. Pack closely in deep dishes or pint bowls. Keep in cold place. Slice thinly. A weight will press it firmer.

HOW TO KEEP SAUSAGE
1840

To put away sausage for a relish next summer, it should be fresh, nicely seasoned, and rather fat. Stuff some in casings, fry, and coil around in a sweet, clean earthen crock. Pour over them the boiling fat that cooked out of them. If that does not entirely cover, add boiling lard. When cold, tie muslin or paper over the top of the crock and keep in dry, cool place. Instead of stuffing the sausage, it may be made into cakes, fried and put up in the same way, but it is apt to absorb more grease. To use, melt the fat and carefully lift with fork into a dripping pan and set in the oven to crisp the skins.

JERKY — BEEF OR VENISON
1850

Take a cut of beef, venison, or other meat except pork. Trim fat from meat. Remove bones. Put meat on a board; sprinkle with salt and pepper and any other spices you desire. Pound in seasoning (or meat may be sliced first, then seasoned). Turn over and repeat salting and pounding.

Prepare pan of water for blanching meat — 1 qt. water and 1 tbsp. salt. Bring to simmer and hold at that temperature while blanching. Cut meat with grain into strips about 1/2-inch thick or less. Dip each into hot water and hold for 10 to 15 seconds until it turns whitish gray. Hang at once by stringing with looped threads from one end. Prevent contamination from flies, dogs, etc. (Cheesecloth not wrapped tightly may be used.)

Drying rate should be high. Should be done in 3 to 5 days. Jerky will be almost black and will break like a twig. Store in covered jars. May be carried in pockets. Stew may be made by breaking into small bits, searing in a little lard or shortening, and adding a little flour, water, and vegetables.

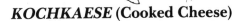

KOCHKAESE (Cooked Cheese)
1854 — Sofie Brandenberger

To 5 gallons farm fresh skimmed milk, add 2 cups clabber. Let stand in crock or unchipped enamel pan until clabber, 1 to 1½ days. Heat clabber over low heat, stirring until it feels very warm. Pour into thin sack and press out whey until dry. Let cheese cool, then run through food grinder or crumble into crock. Add 2 tsp. salt, cover with cloth and a large plate, and set in warm place to process, from 3 to 4 days. May then be cooked over low heat.

LOVE IN DISGUISE
1800

Take two nice fresh lamb hearts and stuff with bread crumbs, sage, and onions. Bake for about 10 minutes in sharp oven, then take some prepared mashed potatoes and cover the hearts all over and put in oven until brown. Make some gravy and serve hot.

MILK GRAVY
1840 — Handed down from Reuben Gage and
Abagail Burleson Gage families

Cook small portion of salt pork or fresh ham in iron skillet. Remove meat and add 4 cups sweet milk to the hot meat grease. Add a pinch of salt and let boil a second. Pour on hot biscuits or hot corn bread. This was served at suppertime for evening meal.

MINCE MEAT
1909 — Ladies Temperance League of Ozona, Texas

2 lbs. of raisins	3 lbs. of apples
3 lbs. of currants	2 oz. of citron
1½ lbs. of lean beef (cooked)	2 oz. of candied peel
3 lbs. of suet	2 oz. of orange peel
2 lbs. of moist sugar	1 oz. of nutmeg

The rind of two lemons, and the juice of one. Half pint of
——(Blank)——. Mix well.

PIGSHEAD HASH

1859 — Mrs. Lel Red Purcell

Boil the head with little salt until very tender, then chop the
meat as other hash. Season with pepper, onions, parsley, sage, if
you like. Return to the fire until the ingredients are well cooked.

ROAST TURKEY

Carefully pluck the bird, singe it with white paper, and wipe it
thoroughly with a cloth; draw it, preserve the liver and gizzard,
and be particular not to break the gall-bag, as no washing will
remove the bitter taste it imparts where it once touches. Wash it
inside well, and wipe it thoroughly with a dry cloth; the outside
merely requires wiping nicely. Cut off the neck close to the back,
but leave enough of the crop-skin to turn over. Break the leg
bones close below the knee, draw out the strings from the thighs,
and flatten the breast bone to make it look plump. Have ready
your dressing of bread crumbs mixed with butter, pepper, salt,
thyme or sweet marjoram; fill the breast with this, and sew the
neck over to the back. Be particular that the turkey is firmly
trussed. Dredge it lightly with flour and put a piece of butter into
the basting-ladle; as the butter melts, baste the bird with it.
When of a nice brown color and well frothed, serve with a tureen
of good brown gravy and one of breadsauce. The liver should be
put under one pinion, and the gizzard under the other. Fried
sausages are a favorite addition to roast turkey; they make a
pretty garnish, besides adding much to the flavor. When these
are not at hand, a few force-meat balls should be placed round
the dish as a garnish. Turkey may also be stuffed with sausage
meat, and a chestnut force-meat with the same sauce is, by many
persons, much esteemed as an accompaniment to this favorite
dish.

SALT PORK

Cut pieces of fresh pork 2 inches thick, 6 inches long, and 4 inches wide. Place a layer of coarse salt in bottom of a crock, lay a layer of pork, and cover with salt. Continue alternating layers of pork and salt until meat is all used up and last piece is covered with salt. Cover crock with a piece of thin white cloth (piece of old sheet is good). Place in a cool spot such as storm cellar or shaded porch corner. Leave for two or three weeks, until salt is melted and all meat is covered with brine. Remove from crock, wash in warm water, dry and hang in kitchen.

SALT PORK AND GRAVY

Slice 1 lb. salt pork thin. Freshen it by putting the slices into cold water and bringing to a boil. Then dry the slices, slit the edge of each slice, and fry to a crisp. Take it out and put on back burner. To 3 or 4 tbsp. of the fat in the pan, add flour and make a roux, of 2 tbsp. flour to 4 of fat. When well blended, add 2 cups of cream. Season with salt and pepper. Serve the pork on a platter and pass the gravy.

SALTING AND SMOKING BACON
1838

For every 100 lbs. of meat, use 8 lbs. of salt, 8 oz. saltpetre, 3 oz. saleratus, 1 qt. of molasses, 2 lbs. of sugar, and water sufficient to cover the meat. Put all together, scald, and skim off whatever impurities rise to the surface. Pack the meat tight in a barrel and pour on the pickle when it is cold. For beef it should be put on hot. Leave the meat in the brine 6 or 8 weeks, then take out and smoke with green hickory or maple wood, if either can be obtained. If the smokehouse is tight and cool the meat may be left hanging in it all summer, or until used; but if there is danger of insects getting at the meat, wrap each piece in good thick brown paper and rub the outside with salt and lime of the consistency of thin lime.

41

SCRAPPLE

1899 — Edna Barnett

Thoroughly clean hog's head; remove eyes and ears. Cover with cold water and cook in large pot until meat falls from the bone. Add salt while cooking. When meat is done remove from pot; bone and chop it fine. Strain broth through a sieve to remove bones, then make the scrapple.

Mix 1¹/₂ cups white cornmeal in 2 cups cold water. Stir well and slowly stir into 1 qt. boiling meat stock broth. Add ¹/₂ tsp. sage and ¹/₂ tsp. black pepper to 2 cups chopped meat and cook until thick. Pack mixture into greased loaf pans and cool until firm. Slice into ¹/₂-inch slices. Dip in flour and fry in small amount of lard until golden brown. Serve for breakfast with eggs, molasses, or honey.

[When butchering hogs, Edna Barnett always made scrapple. She used the remaining meat and broth from the hog's head to make souse or head cheese.]

SOUSE OR HEAD CHEESE

1899 — Edna Barnett

Thoroughly clean hog's head; remove eyes and ears. Cover with cold water and cook in large pot until meat falls from the bone. Add salt while cooking. When meat is done remove from pot; bone and chop it fine. Strain broth through a sieve to remove bones, then make the souse or head cheese.

Mix chopped meat from hog's head with small amount of broth from cooking head. Season with sage and black pepper to taste. Pack in stone crock. Put a plate on top of mixture and weight it down with a clean, large rock. Put in cool place and let set until firm. Makes a delicious luncheon meat.

[Vinegar or pepper sauce on the slices tastes good. An old family favorite, good with fresh bread and fruit.]

42

SMALL BIRDS BAKED IN SWEET POTATOES

Have as many medium-sized sweet potatoes as there are small birds. Boil potatoes for 1 hour. Have the birds plucked, drawn, and washed. Season them with salt and a little pepper, and put soft butter over them. Prepare the sweet potatoes by cutting a thin slice from each end. Scoop out the center of the potatoes, making a cavity large enough to hold a bird. Season the potato with salt, and spread soft butter over the surface. Place the birds in the potato, which should be sitting on end in a shallow pan. Bake in hot oven for 20 minutes. Arrange the potatoes on a hot dish. Serve very hot. Butter must be used generously.

TO BOIL PIGEONS
1830

Scald pigeons, draw them, take the craw out, and wash them in several waters. Cut off the pinions, turn the legs under the wings, dredge them, and put them in soft, cold water. Boil them slowly a quarter of an hour, dish them up, pour over them good melted butter, lay round a little broccoli in bunches, and send butter and parsley in a boat.

TO KEEP HAMS IN SUMMER
1850

There are a number of modes given to keep hams through the warm season free from the attacks of insects. Some bag them and whitewash the bags, which is troublesome and somewhat expensive; some cover them with dry wood ashes and pack them in barrels; some pack them in barrels and cover thoroughly with pine shavings. But we think the best plan of all, and certainly the least expensive with all those who have a smokehouse is to keep them perfectly dark at all times. We have eaten hams so kept 2 years old, and they were among the very best we ever tasted. Uniform darkness is a complete protection against the attacks of insects. So sayeth the editor of the *Germantown Telegraph*.

TO KEEP PORK SWEET FOR A YEAR
1850 — Nancy Leanorah Matthews

Here is a method of packing pork that will make some work, but then it will keep the pork so that it is sweet and palatable: Prepare a brine as strong as boiling water and pure salt will make it and keep it at or near the boiling point. As soon as the pork is dressed, cut it for packing. The flanks and thin parts may be left in pieces somewhat broad if desired, but the thick parts should be in slices not more than 2 inches between the cuts. Have your barrels or packing tubs prepared beforehand. Put as much pork into the boiling brine as it will conveniently hold and let it lie in the hot brine from 3 to 5 minutes, according to the thickness and size of the pieces. Take it out of the brine and pack into the tub and barrel; repeat till the pork is all in. Then pour in the brine hot and put on weights to keep the pork from floating.

TURKEY
1800 — Louise Wischkaemper

To cook an old turkey or other fowl, no flesh, however tough, can resist 5 hours steaming in a closed kettle. A monstrous turkey, whose years were beyond comparison, was once accommodated with a position in a big wash-boiler, turned for the occasion into a steamer by a structure of coarse wire fence netting near the bottom. After half a day spent in the steam bath, it was taken out, disjointed, and the pieces dipped in melted butter, dredged thickly with flour, and then fried in boiling fat, as doughnuts are fried. An epicure would not have disdained the dish.

VENISON ROAST
1840

Wash venison with cold water. Dry well. Rub pure lard all over roast. Pierce roast and insert little slivers of garlic (very little garlic). Put in covered pot with $1^1/_2$ to 2 cups water, a whole onion, and a large sweet potato. Cook in slow oven for 2 to $2^1/_2$ hours. When done, flour well, add 1 tbsp. butter, salt, pepper, a little hot water, and cover roast with gravy.

44

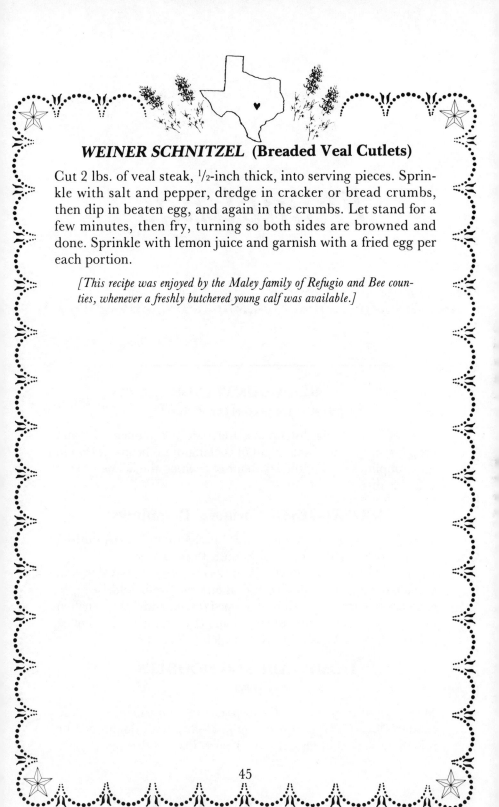

WEINER SCHNITZEL (Breaded Veal Cutlets)

Cut 2 lbs. of veal steak, 1/2-inch thick, into serving pieces. Sprinkle with salt and pepper, dredge in cracker or bread crumbs, then dip in beaten egg, and again in the crumbs. Let stand for a few minutes, then fry, turning so both sides are browned and done. Sprinkle with lemon juice and garnish with a fried egg per each portion.

[This recipe was enjoyed by the Maley family of Refugio and Bee counties, whenever a freshly butchered young calf was available.]

Dumplings

BEAN DUMPLINGS
1890 — Jessie Ethel (Neill) Burns

1 cup of flour, 1 egg, $^1/_3$ cup of water, salt and pepper. Mix and drop by teaspoonfuls into a pot of cooking pinto beans. (Drop in the dumplings during the last hour of cooking the beans.) Serve as a side dish.

MAISKLOESSE (Cornmeal Dumplings)

Slowly add 1 cup cornmeal and 2 tsp. salt to 2 cups boiling water. Cook, stirring constantly until thick. Remove from heat and cool. Sift together $^3/_4$ cup flour, $2^1/_2$ tsp. baking powder, and a pinch of pepper. Add to cornmeal and mix well. Add 1 egg, $^3/_4$ cup cooked corn, 1 tsp. finely chopped onion, and 2 tbsp. melted butter. Shape into balls. Roll in flour. Drop on hot stew, boiled chicken or pork. Cover tightly and cook 12 minutes.

HOMEMADE EGG NOODLES
1850

Mix 1 egg, 2 tbsp. water or 2 tbsp. cream, and $^1/_4$ tsp. salt. Add enough flour (near 1 cup) to egg gradually until dough can be rolled out very thin on a floured board. Place rolled dough on a

towel or paper on table to dry. After dough is dry, cut in thin, narrow strips. To cook, drop noodles into salted boiling water. Cook until desired tenderness; drain. Served with bread crumbs, browned in butter.

HOW TO MAKE VERMICELLI
1826

Beat 2 or 3 fresh eggs light. Make them into a stiff paste with flour, knead it well, and roll it out very thin. Cut it in narrow strips, give them a twist, and dry them quickly on tin sheets. It is an excellent ingredient in most soups, particularly those that are thin. Noodles are made in the same manner, only instead of strips they should be cut in tiny squares and dried.

SUNDAY CHICKEN AND DUMPLINGS
1865 — Asa Wright and John Lloyd Halliburton families

Take a good fat hen or broiler and cut into serving pieces. Cook in large 4-qt. pot, well covered with water. Add 1 tsp. salt and a sprinkle of black pepper. Boil slowly until done. Then add $1/2$ cup milk. Mix up the dumpling batter: Take 3 cups sifted flour and a pinch of salt with 1 tsp. baking powder. Cut in 1 tbsp. butter and add hot water and mix well. Add 1 egg, and then mix and beat batter until creamy. Turn out on floured board and work until it will roll out without being sticky. Roll out and cut into dumplings. Drop them into the chicken broth. When all are dropped, cover with tight lid and simmer for another 10 minutes.

[Very very good — an old family favorite which served as a special Sunday dinner for 3 and 4 generations at least.]

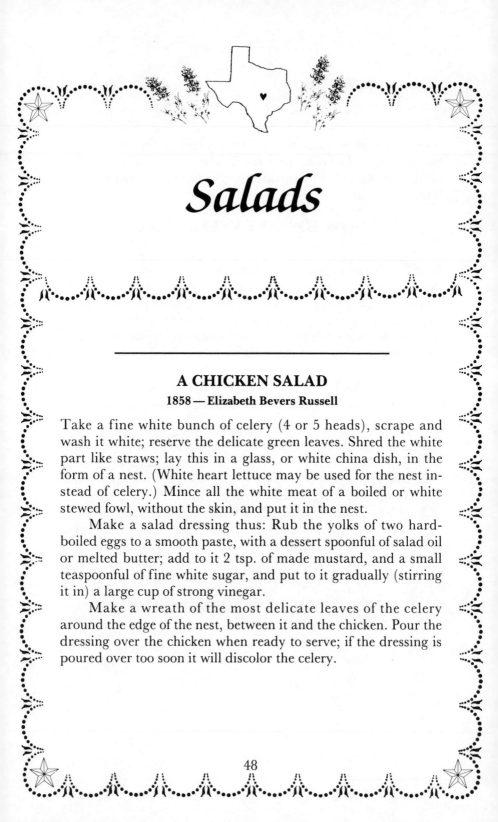

Salads

A CHICKEN SALAD
1858 — Elizabeth Bevers Russell

Take a fine white bunch of celery (4 or 5 heads), scrape and wash it white; reserve the delicate green leaves. Shred the white part like straws; lay this in a glass, or white china dish, in the form of a nest. (White heart lettuce may be used for the nest instead of celery.) Mince all the white meat of a boiled or white stewed fowl, without the skin, and put it in the nest.

Make a salad dressing thus: Rub the yolks of two hard-boiled eggs to a smooth paste, with a dessert spoonful of salad oil or melted butter; add to it 2 tsp. of made mustard, and a small teaspoonful of fine white sugar, and put to it gradually (stirring it in) a large cup of strong vinegar.

Make a wreath of the most delicate leaves of the celery around the edge of the nest, between it and the chicken. Pour the dressing over the chicken when ready to serve; if the dressing is poured over too soon it will discolor the celery.

APPLE SALAD
1860 — Mrs. Joe Lela Duty Nash

Chop together 4 large ripe apples, 1 cup of celery, and 1 cup of nuts. Make a boiled dressing as follows: Yolk of 2 eggs and 1 tsp. mustard, 1 tsp. salt, 2 tsp. sugar, ¼ tsp. pepper, 2 tbsp. butter, 1 cup of sweet cream, and the whites of 2 eggs beaten stiff. Add to the apple mixture.

COLCANNON
1880

Take equal parts of cold cabbage and cold potatoes; cut all together well with a knife. Fry salt pork, and when the pork is crisp, put the cabbage and potato into the fat. Season with pepper and a little more salt, if needed. Cover closely with a plate and let it steam in the pan for ½ hour. Do not stir it until you take it up. Then stir all together and serve hot, with pieces of crisp pork around the edge of the platter. A little onion may be added to this, if liked.

OLD-FASHIONED COLESLAW or "Cold Cabbage"
1871 — Beulah Hancock Harding Hayes

Beat 2 eggs slightly, add ½ cup water, ½ cup cider vinegar, ⅓ cup sugar, 1 tsp. salt, ⅛ tsp. pepper, 1½ tsp. yellow mustard. Cook, stirring until thick. Cool. Combine with 4 cups shredded cabbage. Garnish with fresh cucumbers and hard-cooked egg.

CRESS SALAD
1900

Prepare cress in exactly the same manner as lettuce, washing and bringing to the table firm and crisp. In this salad use for dressing only tarragon vinegar, salt and pepper to taste.

GERMAN POTATO SALAD
1900

Boil medium-sized potatoes with the jackets on. When cool, peel and slice. Fry about half, or one-third, as many onions as potatoes in plenty of butter and lard. When fried, stir in a tablespoon of flour and add vinegar (weakened to suit taste), salt, pepper, and sugar. Pour dressing over the potatoes and mix.

GREEN MAYONNAISE

Chop very fine sufficient parsley to make 1 tablespoon. Put in a bowl and rub with back of spoon until it is a paste. During the rubbing, add 4 or 5 drops of alcohol. Stir it into the mayonnaise and it is ready for use.

HOMEMADE TABLE VINEGAR

Put in an open cask 4 gallons of warm rainwater, 1 gallon of common molasses, and 2 qts. of yeast. Cover the top with thin muslin and leave it in the sun, covering it up at night and when it rains. In 3 or 4 weeks it will be good vinegar. If cider can be used in place of the rainwater, the vinegar will make sooner (it will not take over a week to make a very sharp vinegar). Excellent for pickling purposes.

HYDEN SALAD

1 gallon cabbage, chopped fine	1/2 pint green pepper, chopped fine
1/2 gallon green tomatoes, chopped fine	1 pint onions, chopped fine

Sprinkle salt, and let it stand overnight; next morning pour boiling water over, and squeeze dry. Take:

2 oz. ginger	1 oz. celery seed
4 tbsp. ground mustard	2 lbs. sugar
1 oz. cinnamon	2 spoonfuls salt
1 oz. cloves	1/2 gallon vinegar
2 oz. turmeric	

Boil 10 minutes.

MAYONNAISE DRESSING

1909 — Ladies Temperance League of Ozona, Texas

1 tsp. mustard	2 egg yolks
1 tsp. salt	2 tbsp. lemon juice
1 tsp. powdered sugar	2 tbsp. vinegar
a few grains of cayenne	1½ cups olive oil

Mix dry ingredients, add egg yolk, and when well mixed add ½ tsp. vinegar. Add oil gradually, at first drop by drop, and stir constantly as mixture thickens. Thin with vinegar or lemon juice alternately until all is used, beating all the time. If oil is added too fast the eggs will curdle. A smooth consistency may be restored by adding very slowly the curdled mixture to another egg yolk.

POKE SALAD

Pick and wash leaves of poke salad. Parboil the clean leaves 3 times. Add bacon drippings and salt to taste and cook until tender. Never pick poke salad leaves when berries are on it as it is poisonous then.

SALAD DRESSING WITHOUT OIL

Beat the yolks of 3 eggs until they are light and thick. Add 1 tsp. of dry mustard, 2 tsp. of salt, a speck of cayenne, 2 tbsp. of sugar, 2 tbsp. vinegar, and lastly the whites of eggs beaten stiff. Cook the mixture in a boiler until it thickens, stirring well. It should be as smooth as cream and about the same consistency. Let it get thoroughly cold and put away in glass jars.

WATERCRESS AND LEAF LETTUCE SALAD

1890 — Annie Slaughter

Every spring when the watercress on Honey Creek got just right for eating, my uncle Cub Slaughter would bring Aunt Annie a bucketful. She would go to the garden and pick leaf lettuce and

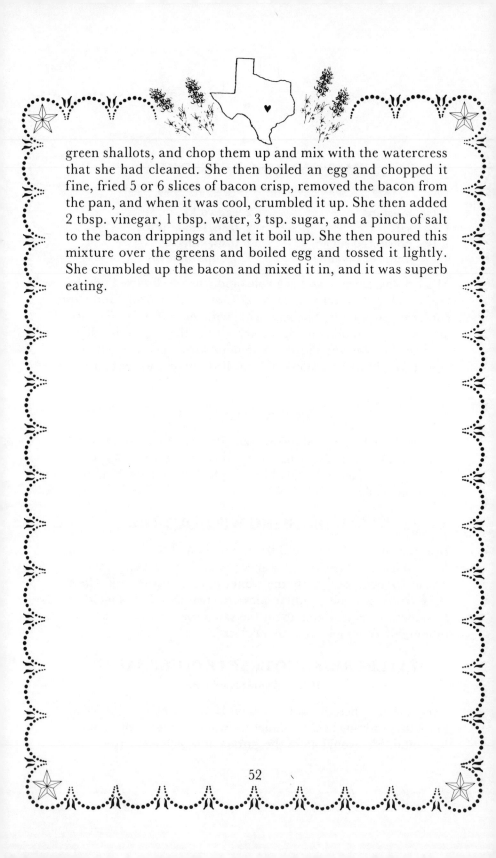

green shallots, and chop them up and mix with the watercress that she had cleaned. She then boiled an egg and chopped it fine, fried 5 or 6 slices of bacon crisp, removed the bacon from the pan, and when it was cool, crumbled it up. She then added 2 tbsp. vinegar, 1 tbsp. water, 3 tsp. sugar, and a pinch of salt to the bacon drippings and let it boil up. She then poured this mixture over the greens and boiled egg and tossed it lightly. She crumbled up the bacon and mixed it in, and it was superb eating.

Vegetables

BOILED ASPARAGUS
1890

Scrape the stems of the asparagus lightly, but make them very clean, throwing them into cold water as you proceed. When all are scraped, tie them in bunches of equal size; cut the hard ends evenly, that all may be of the same length, and put into boiling water. Prepare several slices of delicately browned toast half an inch thick. When the stalks are tender, lift them out and season with pepper and salt. Dip the toast quickly into the liquor in which the asparagus was boiled, and dish the vegetable upon it, the points, or the butts, meeting in the centre of the dish. Pour rich, melted butter over it, and send to the table hot.

BEAN CAKES
1895

Take leftover beans, mash with spoon, add 1 beaten egg, ¹/₂ cup milk, and enough bread crumbs to form into small cakes. Fry.

BOSTON BAKED BEANS

1840 — Nancy Leanorah Matthews

Get a red earthen jar, glazed on the inside. It should be 14 to 16 inches in height, with a wide top. Get the beans at a first-class grocery, lest they should be old or poor of quality. Pick, wash, and soak them overnight in plenty of cold water. Scald them the next day with a teaspoonful of soda; they should not boil unless they have been long stored. Drain off the water, and to 3 pts. of beans (unsoaked) allow a pound and a half of good, sweet salt pork (a rib piece, not too fat is best). Let the beans cover all but the top of the pork, which must be scored; add water enough to cover the beans, in which half a small teacupful of molasses has been dissolved. They should be put in the oven at bedtime, while there is still a moderate fire remaining. They will be ready in the morning. If the pork is not very salty, add some to the water in which the beans are baked.

DRIED LIMA BEANS

At night wash 1 pt. of beans, put them in a small tin pail, pour over them 1 qt. of boiling water, cover closely, and let them stand until 2½ hours before dinner. Then add more water, and let them boil until tender, keeping them well covered with water. When nearly done, throw in 2 even teaspoonfuls of salt; be careful to keep them from breaking. When perfectly soft, drain in the colander, return them to the kettle, and add 3 oz. of butter, ½ tsp. of white pepper, and 1 gill of cream. Shake them about gently and when very hot, serve.

STRING BEANS FOR WINTER

1840 — Nancy Leanorah Matthews

String the beans, but do not break them. Put them on the fire with cold water and allow them to come to a boil. Take them off, put them in a basket, and let them drain until the next day. Make a brine of the water in which they were boiled strong enough to bear an egg. Tie the leaves in a muslin bag, put them

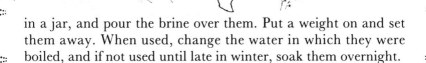

in a jar, and pour the brine over them. Put a weight on and set them away. When used, change the water in which they were boiled, and if not used until late in winter, soak them overnight.

CABBAGE

Nick your cabbage in quarters at the stalk, wash it thoroughly clean, and put it into boiling spring water with a handful of salt and a small pinch of soda. Boil it fast. When done, strain it in a colander. Press it gently; cut it in halves and serve. Greens may be boiled in the same manner, but they should always be boiled by themselves. Should the cabbage be left, it may be chopped, put into a saucepan with a lump of butter, pepper and salt, then made hot and sent to the table.

CORN
1800 — Louise Wischkaemper

Cut the corn from the cob and dry in the oven. Spread 1 inch deep in the pan and stir often to prevent scorching. This will be found better than cooking the corn before cutting from the ear. If the corn is too old for roasting ears, draw the point of the knife through each row of each kernel and scrape out the pulp with the back of the knife. Put in a bag and hang in a dry, cool place to keep. To cook the corn, soak overnight and simmer gently an hour or more. Season with butter, salt, cream, and sugar. If milk is used, roll the bits of butter in flour to supply a slight thickening.

GREEN CORN IN WINTER
1840

Pick the green corn when just right for the table; husk and put the ears for a few minutes into boiling water, just to set the milk in the kernels. Then cut from cob; spread and dry. In the winter take a pint of the dried corn, soak a few hours in warm or cold water, then boil gently and add salt and cream or butter.

BAKED CORN
1855

Do not shuck corn. Place ears in hot ashes, cover with more ashes, then cover with a layer of hot coals. Leave in pit over-night. Remove and eat when hungry.

CORN OYSTERS

6 ears ripe corn, hand-grated	1 tbsp. milk
1 egg	salt and pepper to taste
1 tbsp. flour	1 cup butter

Blend the grated corn, egg, flour, milk, salt, and pepper in bowl. Melt the butter in skillet. When bubbling, drop in the corn bat-ter a teaspoonful at a time and cook until golden colored.

CORN PUDDING
1880

Cut kernels of corn from cob. Stir in 2 eggs, a cup of sweet milk, salt, and pepper. Pour into a pan with butter on top. Bake until firm and brown.

ROASTING EARS
1860 — Ada Lowell Wilson Baldeschwiler

If you will add a cup of sweet milk to the water you boil, roasting ears in it will give them a better flavor.

EGGPLANT, FRIED
1820 — Elizabeth Standifer

Cut in slices half an inch thick and lay in salt water 1 hour; drain, dip in beaten egg, then in cornmeal, cracker crumbs or flour, and fry until brown and tender.

HOMINY FRITTERS
1895

1 pt. hot boiled hominy	1 tbsp. flour
2 eggs	1 tbsp. baking powder.
½ tsp. salt	

Thin with a little cold milk; mix well and fry in deep hot fat to a light brown.

OLD-FASHIONED HOMINY

Old-fashioned hominy or hulled corn is somewhat a different preparation made by soaking the whole grain field corn in water containing a bag of wood ashes. Cook for several hours in a wash pot by placing wood around the pot and stirring the corn with a wooden stick until the grain is tender, and the husk will break away from the kernel. Dip the hominy from the pot with a strainer, place in a large clean container, and rinse through several rinsings until all the ashes are gone. This hominy will keep well if sealed in jars. It may be dried and ground into grits for a breakfast cereal, or fried into fritters; may be served many ways.

HOPPING JOHN

1 cup cooked rice	¼ lb. pork
2 tbsp. butter	Salt, pepper, and butter
2 cups dried peas	

Soak peas overnight. Next day, cook peas until soft, being careful to keep them whole during cooking. Cook piece of pork with peas to add flavor. When peas are cooked sufficiently, there should be only a small quantity of liquor left on them. Mix cooked rice and peas together. Season with salt, pepper, and butter and serve with bread and butter.

KOHL KOPF (Cabbage)
1870 — The Kleburg Family

Select a well-shaped, green head of cabbage. Take out the middle, leaving enough of the outside leaves to stand like a cup. Chop up fine a part of the cabbage you have taken from the inside. Mix with bread crumbs, or crackers, 4 to 5 eggs, small squares of bacon, salt, an onion, and parsley if liked. Put this filling back into the head. Tie in cloth and put in boiling salt water, to boil from 1½ to 2 hours. Serve with drawn butter.

OKRA AND TOMATOES

Peel and slice 6 or 8 tomatoes. Take same amount of tender sliced okra and 1 or 2 sliced green peppers. Stew in porcelain kettle 15 or 20 minutes. Season with butter, pepper, and salt.

ONIONS, BOILED
1890

Skin them carefully and put them to boil. When they have boiled a few minutes, pour off the water, add clean cold water, and then set them to boil again. Pour this away also, and add more cold water; boil till done. This change of waters will make them white and clear, and very mild in flavor. After they are done, pour off all the water, and dress with a little cream, salt, and pepper to taste.

PEAS
1849

To have them in perfection, they must be quite young, gathered in the morning, kept in a cool place, and not shelled until they are to be dressed. Put salt in the water, and when it boils, put in the peas. Boil them quick 20 or 30 minutes, according to their age. Just before they are taken up, add a little mint chopped very fine. Drain all the water from the peas, put in a bit of butter, and serve them up quite hot.

PEAS
1900

To cook peas, throw them, pods and all, into a kettle of boiling water, after washing them and discarding those that are spoiled. When done the pods rise to the surface while the peas stay at the bottom. Peas cooked this way have a fine flavor and are sweeter than when cooked by the usual method.

STEWED PEAS

Take a quart of young, fresh shelled peas. Lay them in a stewpan with 2 oz. of butter (or 3, if they should be old), an onion, cut in fours, a very small sprig of mint, 2 tbsp. of gravy, and 1 tsp. of white sugar. Stew gently until they are tender. Take out the mint and onion, thicken with flour and butter, and serve very hot. Lettuce may be chopped up and stewed with them.

BATTER FRIED POKE
1880

Gather a mess of young poke, wash (3 times), peel, and chop the stems. Beat together ½ cup milk and 2 eggs. Stir into a mixture of 1 cup flour, 1 tsp. baking powder, and ¼ tsp. salt. Dip pieces of poke shoots in beaten egg batter and fry in deep fat until golden brown.

ROTKOHL (Red Cabbage)

In a large saucepan fry 1 medium onion, chopped; add 2 small tart apples that have been peeled and diced, 1 head of shredded red cabbage, 4 tbsp. sugar, salt and pepper to taste, and ½ cup water. Bring to boil; cover and cook gently for 10 minutes. Uncover, stir well; add 4 tbsp. white vinegar and stir again. Cover and simmer for 15 to 20 minutes longer.

FRIED POKE SALLET

Gather a sack full of young tender poke sprouts early in the spring. Wash and parboil them in plain water. Then drain and boil them in salt water. Lift the poke out of water and put in a good hot skillet heated with a little bacon drippings. Cook until grease is absorbed into greens. Serve with boiled egg or add cornmeal to greens and cook until dry. Then break 2 eggs over poke and stir for a couple of minutes. Take up and eat.

STEAMED POTATOES
1865

Put them clean-washed, with their skins on, into a steam sauce-pan and let the water under them be about half boiling. Let them continue to boil rather quickly, until they are done. If the water once relaxes from its heat, the potato is sure to be affected, and to become soddened. A too precipitate boiling is equally disadvantageous, as the higher parts to the surface of the root begin to crack and open, while the center part continues unheated and undecomposed.

WAGON TRAIN BAKED POTATOES
1830 — Sarah Caufield Fullerton

Traveling to Texas and camping along the way, the pioneer woman waited until the fire turned to coals and ashes. She then placed potatoes deep in the warm ashes and went to bed. In the early morning, she had baked potatoes wagon train style.

IRISH SCRAPPLE
1860

white potatoes	cabbage
turnips	large onion
carrots	seasoning

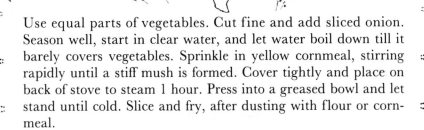

Use equal parts of vegetables. Cut fine and add sliced onion. Season well, start in clear water, and let water boil down till it barely covers vegetables. Sprinkle in yellow cornmeal, stirring rapidly until a stiff mush is formed. Cover tightly and place on back of stove to steam 1 hour. Press into a greased bowl and let stand until cold. Slice and fry, after dusting with flour or cornmeal.

FRIED SWEET POTATOES
1890

Choose large potatoes, half boil them, and then, having taken off the skins, cut the potatoes in slices and fry in butter, or in nice drippings.

STONE CROCK SAUERKRAUT

Remove all green leaves from fresh cabbages; wash, quarter, core, and shred. Pack shredded cabbage in stone crock in about 3-inch layers. Sprinkle with $1/4$ cup salt for each gallon of shredded cabbage. Repeat layers as desired. On top layer place a plate that just fits inside crock opening, weighted down with 10-lb. weight (stones or bricks). Cover with clean cloth and let set in about 70 degrees until it begins to ferment, usually within a day. Then keep in cool, dark place for 8 to 10 days, skimming top daily. Can be kept in crock for several weeks but may also be placed into clean jars and sealed.

BAKED SPINACH

Take 2 lbs. of spinach, washed and with all the stems cut off; steam with a little water and drain. Cut crosswise several times. Add about 2 cups of bread crumbs, 2 or 3 eggs, salt, and pepper. Bake until firm. If you have leftovers such as ham, beef, or cold fried oysters, either grind or chop them and add to the spinach before baking.

FRIED SQUASH
1890

Pare the squash (cut in slices), dip in egg seasoned with pepper and salt, then into cracker dust, and fry to nice brown.

SUCCOTASH
1891 — Georgia Lee Holland-Williams

Take 10 ears of green corn and 1 pt. of lima beans. Cut the corn from the cob and stew gently with the beans until tender. Use as little water as possible. Season with butter, salt, and pepper (milk, if you choose). If a few of the cobs are stewed in the succotash, it will improve the flavor, as there is great sweetness in the cob.

Love Apples
(Tomatoes)

☆   ☆   ☆

A TOMATO CHAPTER
1840 — Nancy Leanorah Matthews

A Newport correspondent of the *Boston Transcript* says that it is a tradition in Newport that tomatoes were first eaten in this country about 1823, in a house still standing on the corner of Corne and Mill streets.

About that time there came here an eccentric Italian painter, Michele Felice Corne. He bought a stable on the street now called for him, fashioned it into a dwelling, and there lived and died. Previous to his coming and long after, tomatoes, then called love apples, were thought to be poisonous. A gentleman told me here today that in 1819 he brought them from South Carolina and planted them in his yard, where they were looked upon as curiosities and prized for their beauty. They became later, however, a very unpleasant missile in the hands of a small boy.

A charming old lady also told me to-day that in 1825 she was sitting with a sick person when someone brought the invalid, as a tempting delicacy, some tomatoes. "Oh, would you poison her?" was the exclamation of the astonished attendants, and yet Corne, in his section of the town, had been serving them for a year previous. As late as 1835 they were regarded as poisonous throughout Conn.

GREEN TOMATO PIE

Use speckless, firm green tomatoes. Cut off stem end. Have pie plate, a deep one, lined with rich biscuit dough. Slice the tomatoes very thin. Fill the plate heaping, grate over about $1/2$ tsp. nutmeg, put in $1/2$ cup butter and a cup of sugar. Sprinkle with a tablespoon flour and turn in $1/2$ cup vinegar. If vinegar is very sharp, use part water. Add top crust and bake in a medium oven for 30 minutes. Serve hot.

GREEN TOMATO PRESERVES
1840

Take 6 lbs. of small green tomatoes, 5 lbs. of sugar, 2 lemons, 1 oz. of ginger root. Parboil your tomatoes in weak vinegar and water, boil and skim your sugar, then add your tomatoes and sliced lemons boiled. Boil your ginger in a small quantity of water, pour it into your boiling sugar, and let all simmer slowly 4 hours.

☆   ☆   ☆

HOW TO PICK A HUSBAND — 1850

If a man wipes his feet on the door-mat, he will make a good domestic husband. If a man in snuffing a candle puts it out, you may be sure he will make a stupid husband. If a man puts his handkerchief on his knee while taking tea, you may be sure he will be a prudent husband. The man who wears rubbers and is careful about wrapping himself up before venturing in the night air not unfrequently makes a good invalid husband, that mostly stops at home, and is easily comforted with slops. The man who watches the kettle, and prevents its boiling over, will not fail in his married state in exercising the same care in always keeping the pot boiling. The man who does not take tea, ill-treats the cat, takes snuff, stands with his back to the fire, is a brute whom I would advise you not to marry upon any circumstances, either for love or money — but most decidedly not for love.

☆   ☆   ☆

OLD VIRGINIA CATSUP
1880

Take a peck of green tomatoes, half a peck of white onions, 3 oz.
of white mustard seed, 1 oz. each of allspice and cloves, half a
pint of mixed mustard, 1 oz. of black pepper, and 1 lb. brown
sugar. Chop the tomatoes and onions, sprinkle with salt, and let
stand 3 hours; drain the water off. Put all in a kettle. Cover with
vinegar, set on the fire, and simmer for 1 hour.

PICCALILLI
1840

Soak a peck of green tomatoes for 24 hours in salt water. Chop
them up quite fine, adding 3 or 4 green peppers, chopped after
removing the seed. Mix them with a teacup of white mustard
seed. Scald enough good vinegar to cover them, spicing it with
pepper, cloves, and allspice tied in a thin bag. Pour the vinegar
upon the tomatoes. Tie up the mouth of the jar in which it is put
away.

PICKLED TOMATOES

Take 1 gallon of green tomatoes and 18 large onions and run
them through your sausage mill. Then take 1 oz. of black pepper,
1 oz. of cloves, 1 oz. of white mustard, salt to taste, one spoonful
of spice. After dripping your tomatoes, and seasoning, cover with
strong vinegar and boil 2 hours slowly. When cold, you will have
as good pickles as you would wish.

RIPE TOMATO PRESERVES
1859 — Lel Red Purcell

Use 7 lbs. of tomatoes, 6 lbs. of sugar, and the juice of 3 lemons.
Peel the tomatoes, and let all stand together overnight; drain off
the syrup and boil it, skimming well, then put in the tomatoes
and boil gently 20 minutes. Take out the tomatoes with the skimmer and spread on dishes to cool. Boil down the syrup until it
thickens. Put preserves in jar and fill up with hot syrup.

SWEET TOMATO RELISH
1900

Mix 2 qts. chopped green tomatoes, 2 chopped green peppers, 2 cups chopped onion, 1 pt. mild vinegar, $1/4$ cup salt, 3 cups sugar, $1/2$ cup pickling spices in bag. Bring to boiling point and cook slowly 30 minutes, stirring occasionally. Remove spice bag. Makes 4 pts.

TOMATOES BAKED WHOLE
1890

Select a number of sound, ripe tomatoes. Cut a round hole in the stem side of each, and stuff it with bread crumbs, nicely peppered and salted. Cover the bottom of the pan with the tomatoes, the opened side upward. Put in a very little water, dredge with flour, and bake till brown. Serve hot.

TOMATO CATSUP
1870

Cut up 1 peck ripe tomatoes and 4 large onions; boil until soft and mash through a sieve. Then add 2 tbsp. each of salt and pepper, 1 tsp. cayenne pepper, 1 tsp. mace, and 2 tbsp. ground mustard. Boil 3 hours slowly, stirring very often, until thickened. Add 2 pts. vinegar and 1 cup brown sugar, and boil 1 hour longer, stirring well. Bottle and seal while hot.

TOMATO OMELET
1880

Take 3 large tomatoes, peeled, cut fine; stew till soft, adding salt and pepper to taste, a small piece of butter, and stir in 3 eggs just as you take it from the fire.

TOMATO CANNING
1840 — Nancy Leanorah Matthews

Tomatoes can be preserved in stone jars with great success. Stew them for 2 hours in the jars. In the oven, or in pans of boiling water, fill them up as the juice evaporates, then cover with a cot-

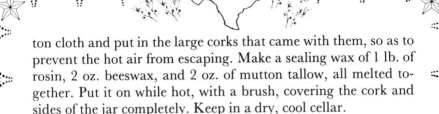

ton cloth and put in the large corks that came with them, so as to prevent the hot air from escaping. Make a sealing wax of 1 lb. of rosin, 2 oz. beeswax, and 2 oz. of mutton tallow, all melted together. Put it on while hot, with a brush, covering the cork and sides of the jar completely. Keep in a dry, cool cellar.

TOMATO SHIRLEY SAUCE
1878

Twelve large, ripe tomatoes, two onions, two red bell peppers, two teacupfuls of vinegar, two tablespoonfuls brown sugar and one of salt. Pare the tomatoes and remove the seeds, also remove the seeds of the peppers, then chop the tomatoes, onions and peppers quite fine, add the other ingredients and boil about five minutes, then bottle and seal.

TOMATO SOUP
1871 — Beulah Harding Hancock Hayes

Empty 1 cup cooked tomatoes into stew pan and heat to boiling and then add pinch of soda. Skim off resulting foam, add 3 cups milk; put in a lump of butter, 1/4 teaspoon salt and a pinch of pepper.

☆　　☆　　☆

TOMATOES AS HEALERS

Tomatoes are a powerful aperient for the liver, a sovereign remedy for dyspepsia and indigestion.

☆　　☆　　☆

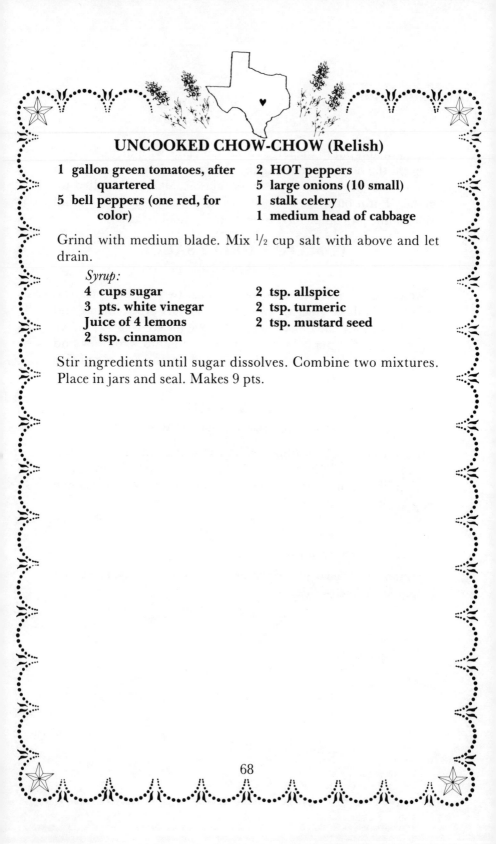

UNCOOKED CHOW-CHOW (Relish)

1 gallon green tomatoes, after quartered
5 bell peppers (one red, for color)

2 HOT peppers
5 large onions (10 small)
1 stalk celery
1 medium head of cabbage

Grind with medium blade. Mix ½ cup salt with above and let drain.

Syrup:
4 cups sugar
3 pts. white vinegar
Juice of 4 lemons
2 tsp. cinnamon

2 tsp. allspice
2 tsp. turmeric
2 tsp. mustard seed

Stir ingredients until sugar dissolves. Combine two mixtures. Place in jars and seal. Makes 9 pts.

Cakes

100-YEAR-OLD POUND CAKE RECIPE

1¹/₂ cups sugar   1¹/₂ cups flour
1 cup eggs   1 cup butter

Mix butter with flour and set aside. In another bowl beat eggs.
Add sugar to eggs while beating very gradually, a teaspoon at a
time. Mix well and bake in a greased and floured tube pan and
bake in oven for 1 hour or when broom straw comes out clean
when inserted in cake.

1-2-3-4 CAKE

1850 — Mrs. Ruth Allen Hancock

Cream 1 cup butter and 2 cups of sugar. Beat 4 eggs and add to
the mixture, beating well. Add 1 cup milk. Mix 4 tsp. of baking
powder with 3 cups of flour; add to the mixture and beat until
smooth. Add 1 tsp. vanilla flavoring or your favorite to the mix.
If nuts or raisins are added to the mixture, then add 2 tbsp. of
flour. Bake in a tube pan for 45 minutes. Ice with your favorite
icing. You may use the same mixture for cupcakes or a layer
cake.

APPLE CAKE

1869 — Elizabeth Ann Mills Roberts

3 apples (cook, drain off
   water, mash fine)
1 cup raisins
1 cup pecans
³/₄ cup butter
2 cups sugar
2 tsp. soda

1 tsp. each of nutmeg,
   cinnamon, allspice, and
   cloves
3 cups flour, sifted
3 large tbsp. cocoa
Pinch of salt
2 eggs

Roll pecans and raisins in a little flour. Mix all ingredients. Bake in tube pan for 1 hour in moderate oven.

> *[Elizabeth Ann Mills Roberts came to Texas in 1880. She boarded the construction crew that built the first Montopolis bridge across the Colorado River at Austin.]*

APPLESAUCE CAKE

1 cup butter
2 cups sugar
3 heaping cups of flour
2 eggs
2 level tsp. soda dissolved in
   ¹/₂ cup hot water

2 cups applesauce
1 cup nuts
1 cup raisins
¹/₂ tsp. cloves
¹/₂ tsp. nutmeg
¹/₂ tsp. cinnamon

Cream butter and sugar. Add eggs. Cream together. Sift flour and spices. Add alternately to creamed mixture with applesauce. Add nuts, raisins, and finally the soda. Bake in buttered cake pans in moderate oven.

Filling:

2 cups sugar
1 cup sweet milk
1 cup nuts

1 cup ground raisins
Butter (size of a walnut)

Cook altogether until thickens. Spread between and on top of applesauce cake.

70

BUTTER CAKE
1855 — Asa Wright and John Lloyd Halliburton families

Cream 1 cup butter until very light. Add 1 cup sugar. Cream and mix well until light and fluffy. Add 1 tsp. any preferred extract, then 2 eggs, one at a time, beating each in well. Add ³/₄ cup milk. Mix well. Add 2 cups flour which has been sifted with 2 tsp. baking powder and ¹/₂ tsp. salt. Pour into well greased and floured cake pans. Bake in moderate oven about 25 minutes. Cool 4 or 5 minutes before removing from pans.

☆　　☆　　☆

A TOPPING TIP

Sift a little flour over cake before icing and it will not run off.

☆　　☆　　☆

CHOCOLATE FUDGE CAKE
(1836 Republic of Texas)
1855 — Asa Wright and John Lloyd Halliburton families

Cream 2 cups sugar and ³/₄ cup butter. Add ¹/₂ cup cocoa, then add ¹/₂ cup buttermilk. Add 2 cups sifted flour and 1 salt spoon of salt, sifted together. Then beat in 2 eggs, add 1 cup boiling water with 1¹/₂ tsp. soda added to it. Beat well. Then add 2 tsp. vanilla. Pour into well-greased and floured cake rounds. Bake in medium oven — not too hot, or too cool, about a 25-minute baking time. Ice with chocolate fudge icing.

Old-Fashioned Cocoa Fudge Icing:

Combine ²/₃ cup cocoa, 3 cups sugar, pinch salt, 1¹/₂ cups milk, 1 tbsp. butter, and some vanilla to taste in heavy saucepan. Bring to bubbling boil, stirring constantly to softball stage. Then beat until fudge thickens. Cool and ice cake.

71

CHOICE CAKE
1845 — Nancy Elizabeth Standifer Davis

1 lb. sugar	1 cup cream
1 lb. flour	1 tsp. saleratus
1/2 lb. butter	Nutmeg to taste
7 eggs	

Beat sugar and butter to a cream, add the eggs, then the cream (with the saleratus dissolved in it), then flour and nutmeg. It requires much beating. Bake in a quick oven.

[*Nancy, a citizen of the Republic of Texas, was born in Bastrop in 1830.*]

COCONUT CAKE
1860 — From Grandmother Matthews's Scrapbook

5 eggs beaten separately, 2 cups of white sugar, 1 of butter, and 4 cups of flour in which 1 tsp. of soda and 2 of cream of tartar have been well beaten. Add the flour to the butter, sugar, and eggs by degrees after they have been well beaten, with 1 cup of new milk. Flavor with lemon or vanilla. Bake in jelly cake pans. Get a box of desiccated coconut; beat the whites of 3 eggs with 1 cup of sugar; spread the icing on and sprinkle with the coconut; add another layer of cake, then the icing and coconut. Put 2 layers of icing and coconut on the last piece. It is delicious and beautiful, resembling a plate of snow, and is often called snow cake.

COUNTRY FAIR CAKE
1884 — Mary Eda Baker Whiddon

1 1/2 cups sifted flour	1/2 cup sifted flour
1 cup sugar	2/3 cup sweet milk
1 tsp. baking powder	2 eggs
1 tsp. salt	1 tsp. vanilla
1/2 cup lard	

Sift together 1 1/2 cups flour, sugar, baking powder, and salt.

Cream lard with ½ cup flour until light and fluffy. Add sifted dry ingredients alternately with milk. Add eggs and vanilla. Beat well. Pour batter into 8x12 pan; bake in moderate oven for 30 minutes, or until light brown. Remove from oven and frost with coconut frosting.

CREAM CAKES
1880

Melt ½ cup of butter in 1 cup of hot water. When boiling, stir in 1 large cup of flour; then take off the stove to cool. When cool, stir in 3 eggs, without beating. Bake 25 minutes in a moderate oven, but not too moderate. The above is just enough for 1 dozen. Do not smooth over on top, but leave as rough as possible. When cold, fill with this cream, that can be made while the cakes are baking: ½ pt. of milk, 1 egg, 3 tbsp. sugar, 2 tbsp. of flavor with lemon or vanilla. Cut a place carefully on one side of the cake to put in filling. If desired, a soft frosting could be added.

DOMINOES (Nice for Children)
1900

Make a plain cake in thin sheets. Cut in shape and size of large dominoes. Frost the top and sides. When hard, draw the lines and dots with a brush and melted chocolate.

EGGLESS SPICE CAKE
1850 — Great Grandmother Sara King Standifer

Take 2 cups raisins and 2 cups water. Cook raisins in water till water is half gone. Mix in 1 cup lard or meat drippings, 2 cups sugar, ½ tsp. salt, 1 tsp. soda, 1 tsp. ginger, ½ tsp. cinnamon, 3 cups flour, ¼ tsp. nutmeg, and nuts if you have them. Bake in moderate oven for about an hour. If you are short a spice or have peanuts, they are good. Being short a spice won't hurt the taste of your cake. Eat plain. It stays moist for a time. This recipe makes good cupcakes or drop cookies.

ELECTION CAKE

1800 — Louise Wischkaemper

This old-fashioned cake, dear to the hearts of our grandmothers, is a troublesome but delicious cake. 5 lbs. of sifted flour, rubbed with 2 lbs. of butter; 2 lbs. of sugar; 1½ pts. homemade yeast; 2 lbs. raisins; 8 tbsp. wine; 8 tbsp. brandy; 4 eggs; 1 qt. of sweet milk; 2 lbs. of currants; 1 lb. of citron; ½ oz. of grated nutmeg. To the butter and flour add ½ the sugar; then the yeast and ½ the milk. Lukewarm in summer; hot in winter. Then add the eggs beaten; then the remainder of milk and wine. Beat well and let rise in a warm place all night. In the morning beat sometime, adding the brandy, sugar, spices and fruit (floured), and let rise again very light. After which put in cake pans, and let rise 10 or 15 minutes. Have the oven about as hot as for bread. This cake will keep any length of time. Temperance people can use 2 extra eggs and 2 wine glasses of rose water to take the place of the liquor, which is as good or better.

FIVE-GENERATION POUND CAKE

1855 — Asa Wright and John Lloyd Halliburton families

Cream 1½ cups butter and 2 cups sugar. Add 7 eggs, one at a time, beating after each. Add 2 tsp. of any extract. Add 2½ cups sifted flour, a little at a time. Add a pinch of salt with flour. Bake in a well-greased, floured pan or deep iron skillet in moderately hot oven. Test with a broom straw. Cool on rack. Will keep for days. This is a Republic of Texas cake.

FRUIT CAKE

1 qt. of flour; 1 qt. of brown sugar; 10 eggs beaten separately; 2 lbs. of raisins; 2 lbs. of currants; ¾ lb. citron; ¾ lb. of butter; 1 tsp. each of cinnamon, clove, nutmeg, and soda; 1 cup molasses; and ½ goblet of brandy or whiskey. Use desired size pans. Bake 3 hours in a slow oven.

[The Ford, Nation, and Cook families came to East Texas in the 1840s. Minnie Ann Nation Cook added walnuts or pecans to her fruit cakes.]

GRANDMOTHER LORD'S PLAIN CAKE

1890 — Jane E. Ray Van Horn and Sharon Ray Verlander Harper

Cream 1⅓ cups sugar with ½ cup lard; add 2 eggs. Mix 2 cups flour, 2½ tsp. baking powder, good-sized pinch of salt, and add to creamed mixture alternately with 1 cup less 2 tbsp. milk with 1½ tsp. vanilla. Makes 2 layers. Bake in moderate heat oven.

[This recipe is from Westhoff, Texas.]

JELLY CAKE
1900

5 eggs	1 tsp. saleratus
1 cup sugar	2 cups sour milk
a little nutmeg	flour

Beat the eggs, sugar, and nutmeg together. Dissolve the saleratus in the milk, and mix. Then stir in flour to make only a thin batter, like pancakes; three or four spoons of the batter to a common round tin. Bake in a quick oven. Three or four of these thin cakes, with jelly between, form one cake, the jelly being spread on while the cake is warm.

LEMON CAKE

Beat 6 eggs, the yolks and whites separately, till in a solid froth; add to the yolks the grated rind of 5 lemons and 6 oz. of sugar dried and sifted. Beat this a quarter of an hour; shake in with the left hand 6 oz. of dried flour; then add the whites of the eggs and the juice of the lemon. When these are well beaten in, put it immediately into the tins and bake it about an hour in a moderately hot oven.

LIGHTNING CAKE

1880 — Nancy Leanorah Matthews

Persons who "just drop in" are a nuisance in the opinion of many housewives, who, nevertheless, will be glad to learn of a cake of which the making and baking occupies only 15 minutes, and which, therefore, will serve to conceal the nakedness of the larder when unexpected guests appear. Take the yolks of 4 eggs, 3 tbsp. of sugar, the same of flour, about 2 tbsp. of milk, and the juice of half a small lemon; the whites of 3 eggs are beaten to a stiff froth and mixed with the yolks, flour, etc., the compound then being put in a buttered pan and placed in a quick oven.

MARBLE CAKE

White batter:

4 egg whites	2 tsp. baking powder
1 cup white sugar	1 tsp. vanilla
1/2 cup butter	2 cups sifted flour
1/2 cup sweet milk	

Dark batter:

4 egg yolks	1 tsp. mace*
1 cup sugar	1/2 tsp. nutmeg
1/2 cup Grandma's cooking molasses	1 tsp. soda dissolved in a little milk (add after flour is stirred in)
1/2 cup butter	
1/2 cup sour milk	1 1/2 cups sifted flour
1 tsp. ground cloves	
1 tsp. cinnamon	*optional

Drop a spoonful of each kind of batter in a well-buttered tube pan — first the light, then the dark. Try to drop it so that the cake will be well streaked through, so that it has the appearance of marble. Bake in a slow oven. Cake may be served without icing, as pound cake.

PECAN CAKE
1899 — Hester Burkett

Cream together 1 cup butter and 1 cup sugar. Mix in 1 cup milk and 5 eggs, beating well after each addition. Add 1 tsp. vanilla essence. Mix 5 cups sifted flour with 2 heaping tsp. baking powder and add to egg mixture. Stir in 8 cups pecans, chopped fine. Stir well and bake in round cake pans in a slow oven. When cool, spread vanilla-pecan filling between layers, and frost with boiled icing.

Vanilla-Pecan Filling:

Mix $1/2$ cup sugar with 2 tbsp. cornstarch and $1/8$ tsp. salt. Add 2 beaten eggs. Pour on 1 cup scalded milk gradually; add 2 tsp. butter. Cook in double boiler until thick and smooth, stirring constantly. Add 1 tsp. vanilla and $1/2$ cup chopped pecans and cool.

Boiled Icing:

Mix $2 1/4$ heaping cups sugar with $3/4$ cup water in saucepan and boil until a thread forms. Then pour slowly into 2 egg whites beaten with 2 tbsp. white corn syrup. Beat until stiff enough to spread on cake.

Hester Burkett's husband, Senator Joe Burkett, along with his brother Omar, discovered the soft-shelled pecan tree that was to revolutionize Texas pecan growing in 1899. Their horticulturist father, J. H. Burkett, propagated the tree into a new variety of paper shell pecans he called "The Burkett." The mother tree still stands at Putnam, Texas. This "recipe," has been handed down for three generations in the Burkett family.

PICCOLOMINI CAKE

1 cup of butter, 3 of sugar, rub them to a cream; then beat 5 eggs very light; stir them gradually into the mixture, together with 4 cups of flour and a cup of sweet milk. Dissolve separately in a little warm water, 1 teaspoonful of cream of tartar and a half teaspoonful of soda. Add a grated nutmeg and a wine glassful of rose-water. Bake in a moderate oven about 15 minutes.

PORK CAKE

Cut fine 1 lb. of salt pork and pour over it 2 cups of boiling water. Add 2 cups molasses and 1 cup of brown sugar. Sift together 7 cups of flour, 2 tbsp. each of cinnamon and allspice, 2 tsp. each of cloves, nutmeg, and soda, and beat into the batter. Add 1 lb. of well-cleaned currants and 1½ lbs. of raisins which have been soaked overnight in 1 cup of brandy. Bake in 3 large loaf pans in a very slow oven for about 1 hour.

☆　　☆　　☆

TO TEST A CAKE FOR DONE-NESS . . .

Most cooks test a cake with a broom splint. Put it in quickly, and if it comes out dry and clean, the cake is done. If cleanliness is desirable, however, it might be suggested that a very good plan is to keep a knitting needle in the kitchen table drawer for testing cake. A sure way of testing cake in the oven is to draw it to the edge of the oven and put the ear close to it. When it is not sufficiently baked, a slight sputtering noise will be heard, but when thoroughly done there will be no sound.

☆　　☆　　☆

POTATO CAKE
1840 — Sarah Rider Beaty

2 cups sugar	1 cup raisins
2 cups flour	1 cup of nuts
1 cup butter	½ cup sweet milk
1 cup potatoes (Irish potatoes cooked and mashed)	½ cup cocoa
4 eggs beaten	2 tsp. baking powder

Cream sugar and butter, add milk, beaten eggs, and potatoes. Mix well. Sift flour, cocoa, and baking powder into first mixture. Add raisins and nuts and mix well. Makes three 9-inch layers. Bake in moderate oven about 30 or 40 minutes. Test with broom straw.

Icing:

1¹/₂ cups sugar and 1 cup sweet milk. Let boil in large, heavy skillet or Dutch oven. Add caramel syrup made by browning ¹/₂ cup sugar and ¹/₂ cup butter. Boil this mixture to softball stage and add raisins (1 cup) and chopped nuts (1 cup). Beat and cover all layers of cake.

POUND CAKE

1 lb. butter	1 lb. flour
1 lb. sugar	¹/₂ tsp. mace
yolks of 10 eggs	2 tbsp. brandy
whites of 10 eggs	

Cream butter and add sugar gradually. Continue beating until smooth, then add egg yolks that have been beaten thick and lemon colored. Beat whites of eggs until stiff and dry. Add to butter mixture along with flour, mace, and brandy. Beat vigorously 5 minutes. Bake in a deep pan in a slow oven.

PRUNE CAKE

1850 — Mrs. Almeda Searborough

Cream 1 cup lard and 2 cups sugar with wooden spoon. Add 3 whole eggs and beat well. Add 1 cup chopped, cooked prunes. Sift together 2 cups flour, 1 tsp. allspice, 1 tsp. ground cloves, 1 tsp. cinnamon, 1 tsp. nutmeg, and 1 tsp. salt. Add 1 cup buttermilk in which you have beaten 1 tsp. soda to creamed mixture. Pour into greased and floured pan. Bake 1 hour and 10 minutes. Put in a covered cake plate to steam.

PUMPKIN CAKE

1850 — Asa Wright and John Lloyd Halliburton families

Sift 2 cups flour, 1 tsp. soda, 1 tsp. allspice, 1 tsp. cinnamon, 1 tsp. cloves, 1 tsp. nutmeg, and ¹/₂ tsp. salt together. Cream ²/₃ cup butter with 2 cups sugar, add 4 eggs, beating after each addition. Mix in 1 cup sweet potatoes or pumpkin and 1 cup buttermilk. Add flour mixture to egg mixture and beat thoroughly. Bake in 3 round cake tins or a loaf pan in a moderate oven.

SHORTCAKES
1850

Use rhubarb, strawberries, peaches, raspberries, or apples. One teacupful sour cream, or butter size of a butternut and teacupful buttermilk, or teaspoonful of cream of tartar and cup of cold water or sweet milk, and half a teaspoonful of saleratus. Flour to roll. Roll ½-inch thick. Bake 20 minutes. Split and butter both sides, fill with berries, and sweeten with white sugar. Serve with cream.

1860 CAKE

2 cups white flour	2 eggs
2 cups white sugar	1 cup buttermilk
1 cup cocoa	2 tsp. baking soda
1 cup water	a pinch salt
¾ cup melted lard	2 tsp. vanilla

Sift the first 3 ingredients together. Add the next 3 and beat well. Then add remaining ingredients. Bake in a moderately hot oven in a long pan. Ice with favorite icing.

[This recipe was handed down in the Nettles family and was prepared by a servant whose reputation for this cake was renowned.]

SPRINGERLE (Anise Cakes)
1850

Beat 4 eggs and add 2 cups sugar and 1 tbsp. butter. Then add about 3½ cups flour and ½ tsp. baking powder to make a stiff dough. On floured board, roll out ⅓-inch thick. Press floured Springerle form or rolling pin on dough and separate the cakes or cut dough into cake sizes. Place on greased cookie sheets which have been sprinkled with anise seed. Let dry overnight. The next day bake in slow oven, until lower part of cake is light yellow. This is usually baked for Christmas.

STACK CAKE
1830 — Margaret Crawford

Cook 3 lbs. dried apples; mash and sweeten. Cream ½ cup butter and 2 cups sugar; add 4 eggs and beat. Add 1 cup milk and 1
tsp. vanilla a little at a time to 4 cups flour mixed with 3 tsp.
baking powder and ¼ tsp. salt. Pinch off dough and roll to ¼
inch. Use plate to cut out rounds, about 10 or 12. Bake on top of
stove on ungreased skillet until brown. Stack cakes or layers,
putting dried apples between each layer. I often use jelly or jam
(any fruit flavor) instead of dried apples.

*[This recipe was brought from St. Joseph, Missouri, by Margaret
Crawford and has been passed down in her family.]*

TO ICE A GREAT CAKE
1805

Take the whites of 24 nice, fresh eggs and a pound of double refined sugar (beat and sifted fine); mix both together in a deep
earthen pan, and with a whisk, whisk it well for 2 or 3 hours till
it looks white and thick. Then, with a thin broad board or a
bunch of clean, white feathers, spread it all over the top and
sides of the cake. Set it at a proper distance before a good, clean
fire, keep turning it continually for fear of its changing color; a
cool oven is best and will harden it. You may perfume the icing
with what perfume you please.

Cookies

ANNA'S TEA CAKES
1875 — Anna Brown Roberts

Mix 1 cup sugar and ½ cup of butter. Add 1 egg and 1 tsp. of vanilla, 2 cups of flour, ½ cup of milk, and 1 tsp. baking powder. Press dough into flat pan and sprinkle sugar over it. Press again. Cook at medium heat.

AUNT SADIE'S HONEY COOKIES
1870 — Sarah Jane (Aunt Sadie) Shelley

Cream 1 cup sugar and 1 cup shortening. Add 1 cup honey, 2 eggs, 1 tsp. soda, a pinch of salt, and mix well. Add just enough flour to make stiff dough. Roll to about ¼- to ½-inch thickness. Cut into shapes desired and bake in a hot oven until brown, about 10 minutes. (If a modern oven is used, about 400 degrees will do.)

[Sarah Jane (Aunt Sadie) Shelley was the daughter of Anderson Campbell Shelley, a pioneer of the Round Mountain Community, Blanco, Texas. Aunt Sadie never married, as her fiancé was killed in an Indian raid when Sadie was a young woman. She lived to be 100 years old. Grandmother Faith Shelley Riley served these cookies to everyone who

stopped by the Riley house in the Lone Grove community. She was famous for Aunt Sadie's Honey Cookies.]

☆　　☆　　☆

COOKIES

"O weary mothers mixing dough,
Don't you wish that food would grow?
Your lips would smile, I know, to see
a cookie bush, or a doughnut tree."

☆　　☆　　☆

COTTAGE CHEESE COOKIES

1/4 cup butter or lard	1 1/2 cups sugar
2 eggs	1 cup cottage cheese
2 cups flour	2 1/2 tbsp. lemon juice
1 tsp. baking powder	2 tsp. grated lemon rind
1 tsp. salt	

Cream shortening and sugar; beat in eggs, lemon juice, and rind. Rub cottage cheese through medium sieve and add. Sift dry ingredients and mix well. Drop by teaspoon to greased cookie tin. Bake in medium hot oven about 15 minutes, until deliciously browned.

FRUIT COOKIES
1868 — Mrs. Joe Lela Duty Nash

1 cup sugar, 1 cup lard or butter, 1 cup chopped raisins, 2 tbsp. sour cream or milk, 1 egg, 1/2 tsp. soda, nutmeg, cinnamon, and whole cloves. Flour enough to roll cookies thin. Cut into rounds. Bake in a quick oven.

GERMAN HONEY COOKIES

Heat 1 1/4 cups honey and 2 cups sugar till sugar is melted. Cool. Add 1 tsp. soda, 3/4 cup liquor, 1 tbsp. nutmeg, 2 tsp. cinnamon, 4 cups flour, and 3 cups chopped nuts. Mix well with hands. Let stand overnight. Roll out on well-floured board and cut into cookie-size shapes. Bake in slow oven until just golden brown. Remove from oven and take out of pan while warm. Store in white flour sack for two weeks in a dark place until they become chewy. Good at Christmastime.

GINGER SNAPS
1850 — Grandmother Matthews

1 cup of lard, 1 cup of molasses, 1 cup of sugar, 1 teaspoonful of ginger, 1 teaspoonful of soda, dissolved in a little water. Boil the sugar, molasses, and lard 5 minutes; let it cool. Then add the other ingredients and flour to make stiff. Bake in a quick oven, and keep in a dry, open place.

GREAT-GRANDMOTHER'S COOKIES
1865 — Asa Wright and John Lloyd Halliburton families

Cream 1 cup lard or butter with 2½ cups sugar. Add ¾ cup sweet milk, 1 tsp. baking powder. Add 5 eggs, beating well after each addition. Add 1 tsp. extract. Add just enough flour to enable dough to be rolled out. Sprinkle with sugar and bake in a fast oven.

[These cookies were first baked on sheet iron used for cookie sheets and baked in a brick oven.]

LECKERLI-SPICED FRUIT SQUARES
(Very Old)

1 cup sugar	1½ oz. candied citron
1 generous cup honey	1 tsp. soda
1½ tsp. ground cloves	2 tbsp. brandy
1½ tbsp. cinnamon	1 egg
¼ tsp. salt	
1 cup pecans	*Icing:*
3 cups flour	½ cup sugar
1½ oz. candied orange peel	¼ cup water

Combine sugar and honey in saucepan. Bring to boiling point,

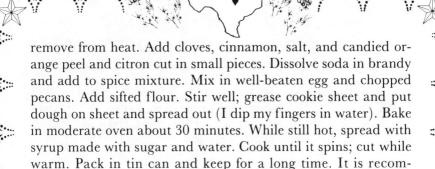

remove from heat. Add cloves, cinnamon, salt, and candied orange peel and citron cut in small pieces. Dissolve soda in brandy and add to spice mixture. Mix in well-beaten egg and chopped pecans. Add sifted flour. Stir well; grease cookie sheet and put dough on sheet and spread out (I dip my fingers in water). Bake in moderate oven about 30 minutes. While still hot, spread with syrup made with sugar and water. Cook until it spins; cut while warm. Pack in tin can and keep for a long time. It is recommended to let them ripen for at least 2 weeks.

LITTLE FRUIT COOKIES
1852 — Anna Vetter, Lydia Vetter

Cream 2 cups sugar and 1 cup butter. Add 2 eggs and beat well. Dissolve 1 tsp. soda in 4 tbsp. sour cream or "milk flour" and add to egg mixture. Sift 2 tsp. cinnamon, 2 tsp. nutmeg, and 1 cup flour together. Dredge 1 cup walnuts and 1 cup currants in flour mixture. Add to first mixture. Add enough additional flour to make a stiff batter. Roll out, cut, and place on greased iron sheet. Bake in moderate oven until golden brown. Raisins and pecans can be used instead of currants and walnuts. These cookies can be prepared by the drop method.

[The original recipe was brought by the Hardt family when they came from Germany.]

MACAROONS, ALMOND OR COCONUT
1900

1 lb. sugar; ¼ lb. blanched and pow'd almonds (or grated coconut); whites of 3 eggs. Mix; sprinkle sugar on white or light brown paper and drop the mixture thereon and bake quickly.

MAPLE SNAPS

1 cup lard or butter, 1 pt. maple syrup, 1 tsp. soda, dissolved in 2 tbsp. of water. Flour enough to make stiff dough. Roll very thin and bake in quick oven.

OLD-TIME MOLASSES COOKIES

Handed down from Reuben Gage and Abagail Burleson Gage families

Mix 2 cups of molasses with 1 cup of sugar and ½ cup of butter. Add 1 tsp. soda, 1 tbsp. ginger, 3 eggs, and ½ cup cold water. Add flour to roll out, but do not roll too thin. Bake in a quick oven.

EGG TEA CAKES

1866 — Luella Jane "Neb" Osborn Fuqua

3 cups sugar	2 cups butter
6 whole eggs	2 tsp. baking soda
2 tbsp. warm water	1 tsp. salt
8 cups flour	

Cream sugar and butter until light and fluffy. Add eggs and mix well. Mix soda with water and add to sugar and butter. Stir in flour by hand. Place small amount of dough on floured board and work in more flour till it's of an easy-working consistency. Roll, cut out, and bake on a greased sheet.

STUFFED TEA CAKES

1899 — Miss Agnes Manford

3 eggs	2 tsp. baking powder
3 cups sugar	1 tsp. vanilla
1 cup butter	flour enough to make a soft
1 cup buttermilk	dough
1 tsp. soda	

Roll out thin and cut. Put two together with the following filling. Bake in a moderate oven.

Filling:

1 cup coconut	½ cup sugar
1 cup pecans	½ cup water
1 cup seeded raisins	1 tbsp. flour

Cook in double boiler until very stiff.

Puddings

ALMOND PUDDING
1879

Blanch 1 lb. of almonds. Pound them with rose water to prevent their oiling. Mix them with 4 crackers, pounded, 6 eggs, a pint of milk or cream, a pound of sugar, half a pound of butter, 4 tbsp. of wine. Bake on a crust.

APPLE SNOWBALLS
1900

Swell rice in milk and strain it off. Having pared and cored apples, put the rice around them, tying each up in a cloth. Put a bit of lemon-peel, a clove, or cinnamon in each and boil them well.

BIRD'S NEST PUDDING

4 large, tart apples	¹/₂ cup seeded raisins
4 eggs, beaten	1 cup sugar
3 cups milk	Pinch nutmeg and salt

Pare and core apples. Place upright in buttered baking dish. Fill holes in apples with raisins. Mix all other ingredients and pour over the apples. Bake in a slow oven until apples are tender and custard looks curdled, about 45 minutes.

BOILED CUSTARD
1900 — Mrs. Bertie Hancock Smith

Divide 9 eggs by separating yolks from the whites. Beat the egg yolks and add 3 cups of sugar gradually. Scald 3 qts. of milk (do not boil); gradually add the egg-sugar mixture and stir. Beat the egg whites until they stand in peaks. Have egg whites ready to fold in the hot mixture. Cool and add vanilla flavoring and nutmeg. Boiled custard may be used in place of eggnog.

☆　　☆　　☆

BOILED CUSTARD ADVICE

My great-aunt, who was born in 1852, was famous for her "boiled custard."

When asked for her recipe, she replied, "Sweeten it to taste, and use all the eggs you can spare."

Hers was delicious!

☆　　☆　　☆

BOILED PUDDING
1846 — Jeannette Dyer Davis

Make up a pint of flour at sunrise, exactly as you would do for bread. See that it rises well. Have a large pot of water boiling; and half an hour before the puddings are to go to the table, make the dough in balls, the size of a goose egg. Throw them in the water, and boil them quickly, keeping the pot covered. They must be torn asunder, as cutting will make them heavy. Eat them with powdered sugar, butter, and grated nutmeg.

BREAD PUDDING
1850 — Asa Wright and John Lloyd Halliburton families

Save all leftover biscuits and stale cake. When enough to make a large bread pudding, soak in enough warm sweet milk to soften. Beat 6 eggs with 2 cups of sugar, add to milk and bread which has been worked and mashed with potato masher until creamy. Mix well. Add 2 tsp. vanilla, bake in slow oven until done, about 1 hour. Serve with boiled icing.

Boiled Icing:

Combine 2 cups sugar, 1/2 cup cream, pinch of salt, teaspoon of vanilla, tablespoon butter. Cook on hot stove, stirring to keep from burning. When at softball stage, remove from stove and beat until creamy.

CARROT PUDDING

1 cup grated or ground raw carrots, 1 cup grated or ground raw potatoes, 1 cup suet, 1 cup chopped raisins, 1 cup chopped currants, 1 cup brown sugar, 2 tbsp. molasses, 1 tsp. soda dissolved in a little hot water, salt to taste, 2 cups flour. Steam 3 hours.

CHESHIRE PUDDING
1865

Make a crust as for a fruit pudding; roll it out to 14 or 15 inches in length and 8 or 9 in width. Spread with raspberry jam or any other preserve of a similar kind, and roll it up in the manner of a collared eel. Wrap a cloth round it two or three times, and tie it tight at each end. Two hours and a quarter will boil it.

CLABBER
1860 — Louise Wischkaemper

In the summer, clabber is usually served for dinner and supper. A particularly nice way of serving this is to have a bowl for each member of the family, into which strain the milk. When it turns into a smooth cake, like blanc-mange, serve in same dish with a little sugar sprinkled over it. This is a really delightful dessert, though so simple.

CLABBER CHEESE
1900 — Mrs. Vivian Buffa Hancock

Put a pan of sour milk in the clabber stage over low heat and let it scald until the whey rises to the top. Be careful that it does not boil, or the curds will become hard and tough. Place a piece of

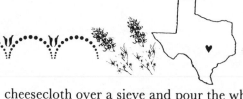

cheesecloth over a sieve and pour the whey and curd into it. Tie it up with a length of cord and hang it on the clothesline for 2 or 3 hours to drain. Next, place it in a dish and crumble it with your fingers. My grandmother fed this mixture to her flock of baby turkeys, but my mother always managed to get into it before the turkeys got any. She added nutmeg to it or put salt and pepper on it. This recipe has been handed down through 3 generations.

CORN PUDDING
1888 — Sophronia Woods Millican

Use 6 to 8 ears of corn, grated and scraped. Boil in half water and half milk until soft. Add 2 eggs, 1/2 cup of flour, butter, and some salt and pepper. Bake about 45 minutes or until firm.

EGG CUSTARD

2 cups sugar
6 tbsp. flour
1/2 tsp. salt
6 egg yolks

6 egg whites
3 cups sweet milk
1 tbsp. vanilla

Mix sugar, flour, and salt together; mix well. Add butter and beat until well mixed. Add the beaten yolks and beat until fluffy. Add the milk and vanilla and mix well. Fold in the well-beaten egg whites until well mixed. Pour into unbaked pie crust. Bake until golden brown.

GREEN CORN PUDDING
1800 — Augusta Below

1 pt. finely cut green corn, 1 pt. of milk, 2 eggs well beaten, 1 tbsp. butter, 1/2 cup sugar, 1 tsp. salt. Melt the butter and mix in the other ingredients. Bake 1/2 hour in oven. If the kernels of green corn are split before cutting from the ear, it will be fine enough. No sauce.

INDIAN PUDDING

1890 — Old Wilson family recipe

Add 5 cups milk to ⅓ cup cornmeal. Cook in double boiler 20 minutes. Add ½ cup molasses, 1 tsp. ginger, 1 tsp. salt, ½ tsp. cinnamon, and pour into greased baking dish. Set in pan of hot water and bake 2 hours. Serve with cream.

NOTTINGHAM PUDDING

1863

Peel 6 good apples; take out the cores with the point of a small knife, but be sure to leave the apples whole. Fill up where the core was taken from with sugar. Place the apples in a pie dish, and pour over them a nice light batter, prepared as for batter pudding. Bake them an hour in a moderate oven.

SUET PUDDING

Sift together:

3 cups flour	**1 tsp. baking soda**
1½ tsp. salt	**½ tsp. ginger**
½ tsp. cloves	**½ tsp. nutmeg**
1 tsp. cinnamon	

Add:

1 cup finely chopped suet	**1 cup milk**
1 cup molasses	**1 cup boiling water**
1½ cups raisins	

Steam 1 hour.

SWEET POTATO CUSTARD

1854 — Eugenia Ellison Brown

Peel, cut, and cook sweet potatoes in a small amount of water. When potatoes are soft, mash thoroughly. Add butter, sugar, and 2 eggs. Pour custard in pie crust and bake until it gets thick.

Pies

AMBER PIE
1845 — Sarah Rider Beaty

Filling: 5 eggs, 1 cup sugar, 1 cup sour cream, 1 cup blackberry jam, 1 tbsp. flour, 1 tsp. vanilla. Beat 4 egg yolks and 1 whole egg together. Add sugar and flour. Beat well. Add jam, cream and vanilla. Mix well and pour into unbaked 10″ pie plate. Bake in moderate but not too moderate oven.

Meringue: 4 egg whites, 5 tbsp. sugar, $1/4$ tsp. cream of tartar, $1/2$ tsp. vanilla. To make meringue, beat egg whites, cream of tartar and vanilla until stiff. Add sugar, one tbsp. at a time, beating well after each addition. Cover top of pie and bake slow till golden brown.

BUTTERMILK CUSTARD PIE
Mary Ann Nelson Pullin

Set a gallon of milk on the back of the stove and when the whey rises, pour all into a cloth bag and hang to drip. To the curd formed add 3 eggs, $1/2$ lb. of sugar, $1/2$ lb. of butter, flavor to taste. Pour into a pricked pie crust, sprinkle with nutmeg, and bake in a moderate oven, until a silver knife tests clean in the custard.

[The Pullins and Nelsons came from Mississippi to Karnes County, Texas, in the 1860s. Grandmother Mary Ann Nelson Pullin always baked custard pie for the Sunday dinner.]

CARAMEL PIE

Put 1 cup sugar in skillet and brown slowly. To 1½ cups sugar add ½ cup flour and mix well. Beat yolks of 5 eggs and add this with 2 cups milk to the sugar and flour gradually — also a pinch of salt, butter size of an egg, and 1 tsp. vanilla. Heat to boiling point and add to melted sugar, stirring constantly. Pour into pastry shell and put on meringue. Cook in a slow oven until brown.

CHERRY PIE

1879

Seed the cherries first, then scald them in their own juice. Sweeten liberally and pour in a deep pie plate lined with a rich paste. Dredge with flour, cover with a top crust, and bake. Scarlet or shortstem cherries are best. It is necessary to scald most fruits, as otherwise the pastry will burn before the fruit is thoroughly done.

CHESS PIE

1850 — Asa Wright and John Lloyd Halliburton families

Cream together 4 eggs, ⅔ cup butter, 1 tbsp. flour, and 2 cups sugar. Add 1 cup milk and 1 tsp. lemon extract. Blend well. Pour into unbaked pie shell and bake in a medium hot oven. Makes 1 large pie.

CHOCOLATE PIE

1894 — Irene Odom Linscomb

¾ cup sugar	2 egg yolks
6 tbsp. flour	1 tsp. vanilla
¼ tsp. salt	1 baked pie crust
3 oz. grated chocolate	½ cup whipping cream
1½ cups milk	

93

Mix sugar, flour, salt, and grated chocolate. Add milk. Cook over hot water, stirring constantly, until thick. Cover; cook 10 minutes. Beat egg yolks; add chocolate mixture. Mix well. Cook over hot water, stirring constantly, for 3 minutes. Cool slightly; add vanilla. Pour into pastry shell. Whip cream, sweeten and flavor. Swirl around edge of filling.

CORNMEAL PIE

1850 — Asa Wright and John Lloyd Halliburton families

Mix 1 cup sugar, 2 eggs, 3 tbsp. meal, 1 tbsp. flour, and a pinch of salt with $1/2$ cup milk and $1/3$ cup melted butter. Mix thoroughly and put in unbaked pie shell. Coconut may be used. Cook in medium oven.

CREAM PEACH PIE

1880 — Grandma Valliant

Pare ripe, juicy peaches and remove the stones. Have your pie dishes ready, lined with a good paste; fill with the peaches. Cover with sugar; slightly butter and then bake without an upper crust. When the pie is done, pour in a cream made of the following ingredients: 1 cup of rich milk put over to boil; stir in the whites of 2 eggs, 1 tbsp. sugar, $1/2$ tsp. corn starch wet up in milk. Boil 3 minutes. The cream must be cold when it goes into the hot pie. Place over the top the white of an egg beaten and sweetened. Return to the oven and brown.

JEFF DAVIS PIE

1850 — Asa Wright and John Lloyd Halliburton families

Combine 2 cups milk and 3 slightly beaten egg yolks. Mix 6 tbsp. flour, $1^1/2$ cups sugar, 1 tbsp. cinnamon, 2 tbsp. butter, $1/4$ tsp. cloves, $1/2$ tsp. nutmeg, $1/2$ tsp. allspice, and $1/4$ tsp. salt. Slowly blend in the liquid to these dry ingredients. When smooth, pour into an unbaked pie shell. Bake in moderate oven until pie is firm. Top with meringue made with 3 egg whites, 6 tbsp. sugar, beaten until stiff peaks form. Brown lightly in a slow oven.

JELLY PIE

4 eggs
1 cup sugar
1 cup jelly

½ cup butter
1 unbaked pie shell

First part: Cream butter and sugar. Add well-beaten egg yolks. Second part: Beat egg whites until peaks are formed. Add jelly and continue beating until well mixed. Fold part 2 into part 1 and pour into shell. Bake in moderate oven, until custard is firm.

[This was a popular recipe in Burnet County, Texas, around the turn of the century.]

LEMON MERINGUE
1879

1 pt. of bread crumbs soaked in 1 qt. of new milk; 1 cup of sugar; yolks of 4 eggs; grated rind of 1 lemon. Beat these ingredients lightly and bake as a custard. Then spread on fruit jelly or stewed apples (fresh). Froth the whites with 4 tbsp. of sugar and juice of the lemon. Spread over the top and brown.

MERINGUE DELIGHT
1900 — Lillie Townsend

Have oven moderate hot. Beat with a fork 2 egg whites to soft stage. Mix ¼ tsp. cream of tartar. Add ¾ cup sugar and beat until stiff. Add almond extract (about ¼ tsp.), 1 tsp. vanilla, and 1 cup any kind chopped nuts. Shave a little chocolate in it. Drop on flat pan. Place in oven and let fire go out. Do not open door until morning.

PASTRY MAKING
1850 — Asa Wright and John Lloyd Halliburton families

Cut in ½ lb. butter (1 cup) and ½ lb. lard (1 cup) into 1 lb. (4 cups) sifted flour. Add 1 cup water (as cold as possible), ½ tsp. salt, and blend until the dough is not sticky, having board and

pin well floured. Divide into 3 parts, then divide each part into 2 parts. Will make 3 double-crust pies or 6 one-crust pies. Bake in hot oven.

[Pastry making was created in Paris in 1270 and extended all over the French Kingdom in 1566. Real pastry, as it is known today, was created about 1790 and was not developed to its present-day standard of proficiency until the beginning of the nineteenth century. Pastry making was introduced in America by the Pilgrims, and its story is closely related to our traditions, customs, and progress.]

PINTO BEAN PIE
Grandmother Raven's cookbook

3 cups of pinto beans, cooked and mashed fine	2 tbsp. butter
4 beating eggs	$^1/_4$ tsp. salt
1$^1/_2$ cups sugar	$^1/_2$ tsp. nutmeg
$^1/_2$ cup sweet milk	$^1/_2$ tsp. cinnamon
	$^1/_2$ tsp. allspice

Mix and bake in uncooked crust.

PUMPKIN PIE
1850 — Asa Wright and John Lloyd Halliburton families

To 2 pts. (4 cups) fresh cooked warm pumpkin add 1 tsp. ginger, $^1/_2$ tsp. cloves, pinch of salt. Mix in 2 cups sugar and 6 well-beaten eggs. Heat a mixture of 1 pt. of new milk and 3 lumps of butter (small egg-size) until butter melts. Add the milk mixture to the pumpkin mixture. This makes 2 large pies. Pour mixture into pie pans which have been lined with pie crust. Bake in medium oven until knife blade comes out clean. Serve with whipped cream.

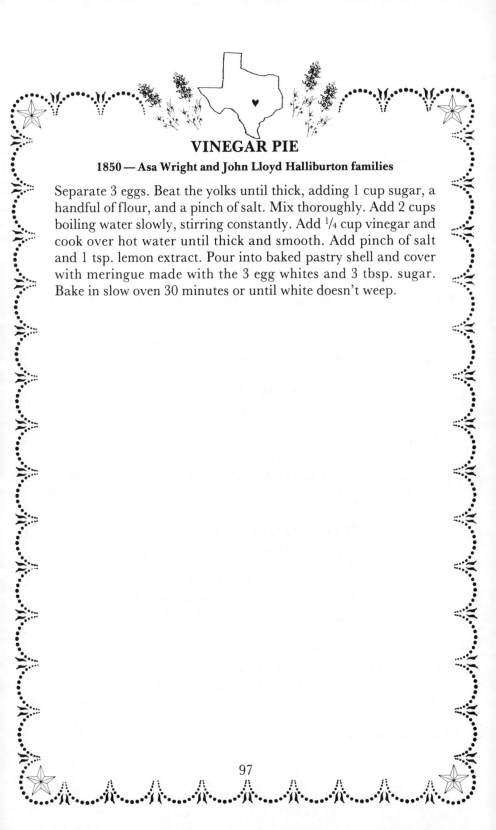

VINEGAR PIE

1850 — Asa Wright and John Lloyd Halliburton families

Separate 3 eggs. Beat the yolks until thick, adding 1 cup sugar, a handful of flour, and a pinch of salt. Mix thoroughly. Add 2 cups boiling water slowly, stirring constantly. Add 1/4 cup vinegar and cook over hot water until thick and smooth. Add pinch of salt and 1 tsp. lemon extract. Pour into baked pastry shell and cover with meringue made with the 3 egg whites and 3 tbsp. sugar. Bake in slow oven 30 minutes or until white doesn't weep.

Candy

CHEWY CANDY

1860 — Handed down in Underwood family

Combine 1 cup grated chocolate, ½ cup butter, ½ cup milk, 1½ cups molasses, 1½ cups sugar. Let cook until soft ball forms in cold water. Pour into medium-sized, buttered pan. Cut into squares.

CHRISTMAS PUDDING CANDY

1852 — Anna Vetter, Lydia Vetter family

Cook 3 cups sugar, 1 cup light cream or milk, and 1 heaping tbsp. butter to softball stage. Beat until creamy; then beat in 1 lb. dates, 1 lb. raisins, 1 lb. figs, and 1 lb. coconut, which have been run through the food chopper. (Can use candied fruitcake mix for part of fruit mixture. It adds color.) Add 1 or 2 cups pecans and 1 tsp. vanilla. When well mixed, roll into logs and wrap in dampened cloth until cool. Remove from cloth, wrap in brown paper (waxed paper can now be used), and put away to ripen. Make at least 2 weeks before you wish to use it. The longer it ages, the better.

CREAM CANDY

Put 2 lbs. of granulated sugar in a saucepan with sufficient cold water to barely cover it; add a piece of butter twice the size of an egg and 2 tbsp. of vinegar. Boil this without stirring, about 25 minutes. Just before removing from the fire, flavor with 1 tsp. of vanilla. Pour into well-greased pans. When cool enough, pull for a few minutes.

HOREHOUND CANDY

1 oz. dried horehound	$^1/_4$ cup light corn syrup
4$^1/_3$ cups light brown sugar, well-packed	1$^1/_2$ cups water

Simmer horehound in the water for about 30 minutes, and strain. To the liquid add the sugar and corn syrup. Cook until brittle stage when tested in cold water. Pour into greased shallow tin pan and as it cools, mark the candy into small squares. Makes about 2 lbs.

[This candy is also a good throat lozenge! Dr. Francis Cates Ford, known as the "Father of Medicine in East Texas," passed this recipe on in his family.]

KISSES
1840

Beat the whites of 4 eggs to a stiff froth. Stir into them a cup and a half of white sugar. Flavor with vanilla or lemon. Drop the mixture on buttered letter paper put in pans or on a slab of wood. Bake in a slow oven until a light yellow. When slightly cool, slip a knife carefully under them and join two together by the unbrowned undersides.

POPCORN BALLS
1900

Pop the corn, avoiding all that is not nicely opened. Place $^1/_2$ of the corn upon a table or in a large dripping pan. Put a little water in a suitable kettle with sugar, 1 lb.; boil as for candy, until it becomes quite waxy in water, then remove from the fire and dip into it 6 to 7 tbsp. of thick gum solution, made by pouring boiling water upon gum arable overnight or some hours before. Now dip the mixture upon different parts of the corn, putting a stick, or the hands, under the corn, lifting up, and mixing until the corn is all saturated with the candy mixture. Then, with the hands, press the corn into balls, as the boys do snowballs, being quick lest it sets before you get through. This amount will make about 100 balls if properly done. White or brown sugar may be used. And for variety, white sugar for a part, and molasses or syrup for another batch. Either of these is suited to street peddlers.

PULLED MOLASSES CANDY

1868 — Mrs. Joe Lela Duty Nash

Boil 1 qt. of molasses in a deep vessel to keep it from boiling over. Boil steadily, stirring from the sides and bottom. When a little poured in a glass of cold water becomes brittle, it is done. Pour it into buttered dish. Wash your hands real clean to be ready to pull the candy. As soon as the cooked molasses is cool enough to handle, roll it in a long roll. Pull the roll into a long ropelike length. Then fold it back to half the length, roll it together, and pull it again. This is called "pulling the candy." Keep pulling the candy until it changes to a light color but is still soft enough to handle. Pull to a long ropelike length, cut in 6-inch lengths, and twist. This candy looks like stick candy.

SEA FOAM CANDY

1880s

2 cups brown sugar	1 tsp. vanilla
1/2 cup water	1/2 cup nutmeats
1 egg white	

Boil sugar and water together until it forms a ball when dropped in cold water. Pour syrup slowly into stiffly beaten egg white. Beat until stiff. Drop by spoonfuls on wax paper. Make on a fair day.

Canning and Pickling

CANNING CORN
1860

Fill the cans with the uncooked corn (freshly gathered), cut from the cob, and seal them hermetically. Surround them with straw to prevent them striking against each other and put them into a boiler over the fire, with enough cold water to cover them. Heat the water gradually; when they have boiled an hour and a half, puncture the tips of the can to allow the escape of gases. Seal them immediately while they are still hot. Continue to boil them for 2½ hours. In packing the cut corn in the can, the liberated milk and juices surround the kernels, forming a liquid in which they are cooked. This process is the very best for preserving the natural flavor of green corn.

CANNING GREEN BEANS
1868 — Mrs. Joe Lela Duty Nash

String and snap 6 qts. of green beans as for the table. Boil for 1 hour, using enough water to cover them well. Salt to taste, then add 1 cup sugar and 1½ cups of vinegar. Boil 30 minutes longer. Can while hot, being sure to have the beans in the jar well cov-

ered with the water in which they were cooked and seal. They are sure to keep and are sure fine eaten cold fresh from the jar, or they may be cooked again and seasoned in any way preferred.

CORN VINEGAR
1830 — Nancy Elizabeth Standifer Davis

Cut off of the cob 1 pt. of corn, then take 1 pt. of brown sugar or molasses to 1 gal. of rain water; add the corn. Put into a jar, cover with a cloth, set in the sun, and in 3 weeks you will have good vinegar.

DILL PICKLES
1850

Select cucumbers about the size for dill pickles. Soak overnight in cold water. Pack pickles with dill in old-fashioned crock. Boil up 3 qts. water, 1 qt. vinegar, and 1 cup pickling salt. Pour over cucumbers and seal in crock.

[This recipe was handed down in the Richardson family of Lockhart, Texas.]

MIXED PICKLES
1850

Take equal quantities of onions, cucumbers, small green tomatoes, and cauliflowers; put them in a porcelain kettle in cold, salt water. Set the kettle on the stove and let them just begin to boil, then pack in glass jars, a few of each alternately and about three green or red peppers to each quart, and a gill of white mustard seed, then fill the jar with hot vinegar and seal.

QUICK PICKLED BEETS
1895

Take 12 small whole cooked beets or 4 cups sliced cooked beets. Empty into saucepan. Add ¹/₂ cup vinegar (5%) and ¹/₂ cup sugar. Stir gently until sugar is dissolved. Add 3 bay leaves, 1 tsp. whole black pepper, and 1 tsp. whole cloves tied in a thin cloth. Heat to boiling; simmer until beets are heated through. Chill a while for spices to season.

SMALL CUCUMBER PICKLES
1886 — Mrs. S. T. Rorer

Wash and wipe 100 small cucumbers and place them in jars. Cover them with boiling brine, strong enough to bear an egg; let stand 24 hours. Then take them out, wipe, place in clean jars, and cover with hot vinegar, spiced with an onion, 12 whole cloves, 1 oz. of mustard seed, and 3 blades of mace. They will be ready to use in 2 weeks.

SWEET PICKLES
1890

After eating watermelons, take the rind, and with a sharp knife pare off the outside green and all the heart. Cut the white firm part into strips 2 inches long. Make a syrup by putting 1 qt. vinegar and 1 lb. sugar on the stove to boil; 2 oz. cloves tied in a cloth, and $1/2$ oz. allspice (ground); add quart of water. When well boiled, skim and place your rind in the syrup. Let boil till each piece looks clear and is tender. Skim out into a jar and add more rind. When done, set away to cool, and in 2 or 3 days I would like to come and help you eat them.

WATERMELON RIND PICKLES
1850 — Edna Rogers

Peel rinds; leave a little red on. Cut in size desired. Soak in solution of $1/4$ cup coarse salt and 1 qt. water for 2 hours. Rinse well; put on to boil in cold water. Cook 10 minutes or until tender. Prepare syrup of 7 cups white sugar, 2 cups white vinegar, scant $1/2$ tsp. oil of cloves and $1/2$ tsp. oil of cinnamon. Bring syrup to a boil; pour over cooked rinds. Let stand overnight and next day drain off syrup and cook up and pour over rind again. The third

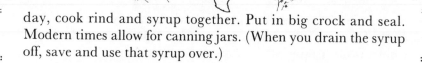

day, cook rind and syrup together. Put in big crock and seal. Modern times allow for canning jars. (When you drain the syrup off, save and use that syrup over.)

PICKLED VEAL OR BEEF
1900

Rub each piece of beef or veal very lightly with salt. Let them lie singly on a tray or board for 24 hours, then wipe very dry. Pack closely in a barrel or keg, being sure that it is perfectly sweet and clean. Have the pickle ready and made thus: boil 4 gallons of soft water with 10 lbs. of coarse salt, 4 oz. of saltpeter, and 1 lb. of coarse brown sugar. Boil 15 minutes and skim, while boiling, very clean. When perfectly cold, pour it on the meat, laying a weight on top of the meat to keep it under the pickle. This quantity is sufficient for 100 lbs. of meat when closely packed.

HOW TO CAN FRUIT
1850

Glass and stone jars are the only kinds to use (for the acid of fruits will not be healthful if preserved in tin), and they can be purchased very cheaply. Nearly all the fruits retain their flavor better if they are steamed instead of stewed, as they are not so much broken up. To 4 lbs. of the fruit, take 1 lb. of lump sugar, as it is less subject to adulteration. Fill the jars within 2 inches of the top with the fruit. Melt the sugar in very little water and turn it boiling hot upon the fruit. Place the jars in a pan of boiling water and let them steam about 10 minutes, or until the fruit, by the expulsion of the cold air, has been forced to the top of the jar. Put the cover on at once, with a cloth, so as not to burn your hands, and screw it down tightly while in the boiling water. Set the jars on the table to cool, and if any bubbles appear in them, take off the covers and boil again until the fruit is again forced upwards. Fruit canned in this manner will keep for years and retain its flavor perfectly.

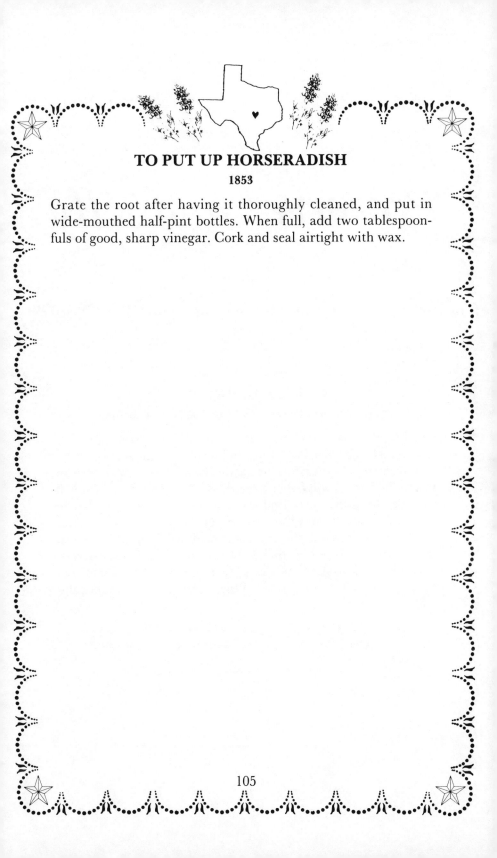

TO PUT UP HORSERADISH
1853

Grate the root after having it thoroughly cleaned, and put in wide-mouthed half-pint bottles. When full, add two tablespoon-fuls of good, sharp vinegar. Cork and seal airtight with wax.

Preserves and Jelly

AGARITA BERRY JELLY
1865 — Asa Wright and John Lloyd Halliburton families

The bright red agarita berry makes one of the most unusual jellies — very delicious. About the middle of May the just ripe berries are ready to thrash. Place a sheet under the bush, spread where the berries will fall into the sheet. When the berries are all thrashed from the bush, find a convenient place where you can drop a few berries at a time in front of a fan, where the berries will fall into a box and the leaves and chaff will blow away. Wash the berries thoroughly; pick completely clean. Cook berries; mash. Strain juice from berries — 1 cup juice to 1 cup sugar. Let cook 25 minutes at a hard boil. When it jells, pour into jars and seal.

[This is a very special recipe, made by five generations. When there is a good berry season these berries can be gathered in supplies to last for 2 or 3 years.]

APPLE BUTTER
1840 — From Grandmother Matthews's Scrapbook

Take 9 gallons of cider, boil down to 3 gallons, then add to the boiling cider about 3 gallons of apples that have been pared and quartered; boil rapidly for about 2 hours without ceasing, to prevent the apples from sinking. By this time they are well reduced and will begin to sink. Thus far no stirring has been done but must be commenced as soon as the apples begin to sink or they will scorch. Spice to suit taste. Stir without ceasing until it is reduced to a thick smooth pulp, which will take about half an hour. I have kept apple butter made in this way perfectly good at 2 years old, without sealing, and it is as good if not a better article than that made in the usual way. Many housekeepers will be astonished at the idea of apple butter and only half an hour's stirring, when they have been in the habit of being over a hot fire all day.

APPLE JELLY
1864 Diary of Civil War — W. B. Gowen

Take juicy apples, cut in pieces; add water to just cover. Then stir gently till tender. Turn into a bag or strainer of cloth. Drain overnight or for several hours. Then put back on stove. Heat and skim. Add ³/₄ pt. of sugar to 1 pt. of juice and heat about 10 minutes.

APPLE MARMALADE

Scald apples till they will pulp from the core. Then take an equal weight of sugar in large lumps, dip them in water, and boil till it can be well skimmed and is a thick syrup. Add to it the pulp, and simmer it on a quick fire a quarter of an hour. Grate a little lemon peel before boiling, but if too much it will be bitter.

CITRON
1840 — Mrs. Elizabeth Scott Stewart Miller

Cover the rind of the fruit with salt water for 12 hours, then with fresh water until the salt is out; then scald in alum water; then in clear water until alum is out. Have ready a strong ginger tea and

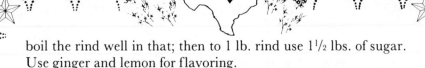

boil the rind well in that; then to 1 lb. rind use 1½ lbs. of sugar. Use ginger and lemon for flavoring.

[Mrs. Miller, born in Pennsylvania in 1825 as Miss Stewart, married Dr. James W. Miller, D.D., first ordained Presbyterian pastor in Texas. He first came to Texas in 1844.]

GRAPE JELLY
1840 — Mrs. Rebecca Stuart Red

Cover the grapes with water and boil 30 minutes, bruising them with ladle until the juice runs freely; then strain through a flannel bag and measure 1 pt. of juice for 1 lb. of sugar. Boil the juice 15 or 20 minutes before putting in the sugar. After adding the sugar, let it boil 5 minutes. Fruit not perfectly ripe will make the best jelly. Do not take the grapes from the bunches, but pick free from dirt and trash.

[Miss Rebecca Stuart was the first female teacher to come to Texas with a four-year college diploma and teach college courses in Texas.]

GREEN GRAPE CATSUP
1895

Take 5 lbs. green mustang grapes. Grapes are best when seeds have not formed. If grapes are old, it is best to cook them first and run them through a sieve before weighing. Add 3 lbs. sugar and 1 pt. vinegar to grapes in large pot. Add 1 tsp. each of cinnamon, cloves, allspice, and salt. Stir and add ½ tsp. red pepper. Cook slow; simmer until syrupy. This is good on meat, beans, etc.

HOW TO PRESERVE A HUSBAND — Circa 1899

Be careful in your selection; do not choose too young and take only such varieties as have been reared in a good moral atmosphere. When once decided upon and settled, let that part remain forever settled and give your entire thought to preparation for domestic use. Some insist on keeping them in a pickle, while others are constantly getting them into hot water. Even poor varieties may be made sweet, tender, and good by garnishing them with patience, sweetened with smiles and flavored with kisses to taste. Then wrap well in a mantle of charity, keep warm with a steady fire of domestic devotion, and serve with peaches and cream. When thus prepared, they will keep for years.

MUSKMELON PRESERVES
1840

Take ripe muskmelons, remove seeds and peel, and cut in pieces. Put into a stone jar and cover with scalding vinegar; let them stand until the next day. Pour off the vinegar; heat it and pour on them again. Do the same every day until the fourth day. Weigh the melon, and to every 5 lbs. add 3 lbs. of white sugar and 1 qt. of the vinegar, and spice to suit. Put all together and simmer till tender. The next day but one, pour off the syrup and boil it down so there will be just enough to cover the melon. You may think it will be a tiresome job, but if you try it you will be well pleased with it.

PEACH BUTTER
1900 — Lula Stanley Rawls

Take freshly washed peach peelings and lay them on a clean towel on top of the roof of the house. Leave them there for one week in the summertime. If it rains, bring them in until it stops. To each quart of peach peelings, add 1½ cups sugar, 1 tsp. cinnamon, and 1 tsp. crushed cloves. Boil it in 1 qt. of water for 45 minutes. Pour up in Mason jars.

PEACH MARMALADE
1840 — Mrs. Rebecca Stuart Red

Marmalade may be made without peeling the peaches. Soft peaches are best. Cut the fruit from the stones and weigh; allow ³/₄ lb. of sugar to 1 lb. of fruit. Put the fruit into a preserving kettle, having first mashed it well — do not add water. Let the peaches boil until clear, stirring to prevent burning, then add the sugar and cook thoroughly. Put into bowls and seal like jelly. Do not strain, for if well cooked there will be no trace of the skins.

PEAR PRESERVES

4 lbs. pears   **3 lbs. pure cane sugar**
3 cups water

Cut pears in half; remove core and pare. If pears are very hard, boil first in clear water until tender; drain. Make a thick syrup of the water and pure cane sugar. Add pears and cook until clear and transparent. Remove from fire and allow to stand overnight. Pack in sterilized jars and seal.

PRESERVED PLUMS

Green gages or large purple plums make the finest preserves. Weigh the fruit and prick in 2 places with a sharp-tined steel fork. Lay the plums in a preserving kettle, alternately with layers of sugar, allowing pound for pound. Heat slowly to a boil, then, very carefully, with a perforated skimmer remove the plums and spread upon flat dishes in the sun. Boil the syrup until thick and clear; return the plums to this and boil 15 minutes. Spread out again until cool and firm, keeping the syrup hot on the fire. Fill the jars two-thirds full, pour on the scalding syrup, cover to keep in the heat, and when cold tie up. If airtight cans are used, seal up when hot.

PRESERVED WHOLE STRAWBERRIES
1900

Mash a quantity of strawberries and simmer for 20 minutes without sugar. To each pint of the strained juice, allow a pint of sugar. Heat the sugar and add to the strained juice after it has been returned to the stove and reached the boiling point; skim and boil until thick. Pour over the hulled berries already placed in heated glasses; or pour the syrup into the heated glasses and drop in the hulled berries (not too many berries in each glass). When cold, tie up with brandied paper and set in the sun daily for 30 days.

POKE PICKLES
1880

Using tender poke shoots, remove leaves and skins. Boil about 2 dozen poke stems about 2½ inches long in salted water until tender. Drain and place in jars. Boil together 1 tbsp. salt, ½ cup water, and ½ cup vinegar and pour over stems. Seal jars.

PRICKLY PEAR JELLY
1852 — Anna Vetter, Lydia Vetter

Gather about a half-bushel of dark red or purple prickly pear apples. My grandfather Hardt always built a small fire and singed the thorns off by putting the apples on a long-handled fork and holding them over the flames. Then the residue of the thorns was cut off before the apples were washed and quartered. Put apples in a kettle or large pot, cover with water, and boil for about 20 minutes. Press the pulp through four thicknesses of cheesecloth and let the juice drip from jelly bag. Grandmother Vetter saved her sugar sacks for jelly bags. For each 4 cups of juice, use 1³/₄ oz. boiled-down strained grape or pear juice, and let it dry some in a cool place. Bring to rough boil. Add 3½ lbs. of sugar (7 cups) and bring back to a hard boil for 5 minutes. Skim and pour into clean jars. Let set for a spell and then cover with hot beeswax.

I remember that after the beeswax or paraffin had set, my

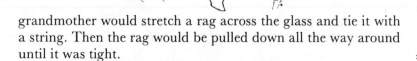

grandmother would stretch a rag across the glass and tie it with a string. Then the rag would be pulled down all the way around until it was tight.

PUMPKIN CHIP PRESERVES

Cut slices from a fine, high-colored pumpkin; peel and cut into thin chips. Of the pumpkin, take 2 cups and put into a broad pan, laying 2 cups sugar among it. Add 1 lemon, sliced thin, and let set all night. Early in the morning, put the whole into a pre-serving pan. Add 1 stick cinnamon, 1 tsp. whole cloves, and 1 cup water. Boil all together until the chips are clear and crisp and the syrup is thick. Half an hour's boiling is generally suffi-cient. Seal in jars. Makes 2 half-pints.

RED CAR MARMALADE
1880

4 oranges (Jaffe, if available)　　4 pts. water (2 qts.)
4 lemons　　　　　　　　　　　　sugar
1 grapefruit

Wash fruit, put in pan with water, and boil for 15 minutes. Cut fruit in half, remove seeds, and put through mincer. Return pulp to the water in which the fruit was boiled. For every cup of liquid and pulp, add 1 cup of sugar. Boil for 45 minutes, when it will jell nicely.

WATERMELON PRESERVES
1900 — Mrs. Vivian Buffa Hancock

Take a thick-skinned watermelon, eat the middle red meat, trim the outside green rind off, leaving the white with a touch of the red. Cut into strips about 1½ inches thick. Lay out on a platter or tin pan, then place it on the roof of the house and leave it for 3 days. Bring it into the house and weigh. Add an equal amount of sugar for each pound of fruit. For a large batch of fruit, add 1 thinly sliced lemon. Cook until a clear syrup is made. Pack into jars immediately. This recipe has been handed down through three generations.

Miscellaneous

BABY FOOD

Babies of 6 months may have beef tea or mutton broth once a day; at 10 or 12 months old they may have a piece of bread or of rare beefsteak to suck. This with bread and milk, oatmeal porridge, or boiled rice and milk is the best diet for a baby under 2 years old.

BAKING POWDER

It is used so very much now, and what we buy is so highly adulterated with alum that it isn't fit to use. You can get the following receipt filled at the drugstore for 30 cents: 16 oz. cornstarch, 8 oz. bicarbonate of soda, 5 oz. tartaric acid. Mix thoroughly, and put through a sieve several times. Place in glass cans, cover closely, and keep in a dry place. This makes nearly 2 qts. and you need not use so much at a time as you do of that you buy.

BANANA FRITTERS
1900

Make a batter of 1 cup warm sweet milk, a large teaspoonful of baking powder, sifted with 2 cups flour, 2 eggs (yolks and whites beaten separately), 1 tablespoonful sugar, and a saltspoon of

113

salt. Stir all together. Dip slices of banana into the batter and drop into boiling hot lard, in large spoonfuls, and fry (like doughnuts) to light brown. Sprinkle with powdered sugar or serve with sauce. Apples, peaches, sliced oranges, etc., can be used in the same way.

CANDIED FRUIT

Dissolve ½ lb. lump sugar in a cup of water; stir slowly, until the sugar is melted, meanwhile heating slowly. As soon as the mixture gets quite hot, the stirring must be stopped until it has boiled violently for 6 minutes, when it is to be set to one side. To drop fruit, string a few pieces on silk or cotton thread; suspend them long enough in the cooling mixture to get them well coated; lift out and stretch string between two nails tacked in a corner, placing a sheet of paper beneath to catch drippings.

CORNSTARCH

Take tender young roasting ears and after cleaning carefully with a sharp knife, cut the grains close to the cob. Wash the grains thoroughly in clean water; remove grains from water without disturbing flour-like sediments settling on the bottom of pan. After the starch on the bottom of the pan has 'set,' drain water from the pan, and place the pan in the sun to dry the cornstarch thoroughly. When dry, the starch may be used to thicken gravies or used in the ordinary manner for starching clothes.

CURD OR COTTAGE CHEESE

Set a gallon or more of clabbered milk on the stove hearth or in the oven after cooking a meal, leaving the door open; turn it around frequently and cut the curd in squares with a knife, stirring gently now and then till about as warm as the finger will bear, and the whey shows all around the curd. Pour all into a coarse bag and hang to drain in a cool place for 3 or 4 hours or overnight if made in the evening. When wanted, turn from the bag, chop rather coarse with a knife, and dress with salt, pepper, and sweet cream. Some mash and rub thoroughly with the cream. Others dress with sugar, cream, and a little nutmeg, omitting the salt and pepper.

FIG FRITTERS
1840 — Asa Wright and John Lloyd Halliburton families

Mix 1½ cups flour, 1 cup sugar, 2 tsp. baking powder, and pinch of salt together. Add 2 eggs and ⅔ cup milk, using enough milk to make a light drop batter. Slice or chop 1 cup steamed dried figs and stir them into the batter. If desired, a few drops of vanilla extract may be added. Drop the mixture from the tip of a tablespoon into deep hot fat and fry golden brown on all sides. Serve as hot as possible with whipped cream or hard sauce.

Hard Sauce:
Cream 1 cup butter until light, gradually beating in ½ cup sugar. Add flavoring extract to please. Sugar may be granulated or brown. 1 tsp. cream may be added to make creamy. Boil about 5 minutes. The longer the beating, the creamier the sauce.

GRANDDAD'S SNACK
1830 — Nancy Elizabeth Standifer Davis

Pour molasses on plate and mix with hot biscuits.

LEMON FRUIT DRESSING
1900

Beat 1½ cups sugar with the juice of 1½ lemons and 2 eggs. Cook in double boiler until thickened. When cool, pour over fruit.

MOLASSES DOUGHNUTS

Beat 1 egg and ½ cup of sugar well together. Add 1 cup of molasses and 1 cup of sour milk, in which 1 tsp. of soda has been dissolved. Stir well together and add 2 dessert spoons of melted but-

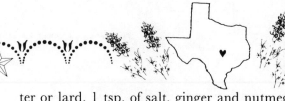

ter or lard, 1 tsp. of salt, ginger and nutmeg, $^1/_2$ tsp. each, and flour to roll. The fat does not need to be so hot for molasses doughnuts as for those made of sugar.

MUSTARD DRESSING FOR FRUIT SALAD

$^1/_2$ tsp. salt	1 tbsp. sugar
1 tsp. mustard	2 yolks of eggs
1 tsp. flour	$^3/_4$ cup of rich sweet milk
2 tbsp. butter	$^1/_4$ cup of vinegar

Mix all together and put in double boiler to cook.

RUMTOPF
1862 — Martha Koehler

Clean fruit in season (peaches, pears, apricots, cherries). Use large crock with fitting lid. Put fruit in crock and add equal amount of sugar and enough rum to cover fruit. Stir. Cover container and let sit in pantry. Add another fruit as they come into season with equal amount of sugar and enough rum to keep well covered. Stir mixture with each addition and in between. After last variety of fruit has been added, *Rumtopf* must sit at least 6 weeks before ready to eat.

[This is an old German recipe and a special dessert at Christmastime in Germany.]

SICK ROOM EGG CUSTARD
1855 — Asa Wright and John Lloyd Halliburton families

Beat well 5 eggs. Take $2^1/_2$ cups milk and heat to boiling point; add slowly to eggs. Continue beating and gradually add 1 cup sugar, 1 tbsp. of vanilla extract, and a pinch of salt. Pour into baking dish and set in a pan of water. Place in oven (medium hot); cook until broom straw comes out clean.

[This custard is very good for a diet in the sick room.]

STALE BREAD
1850 — Grandmother Matthews's Scrapbook

Every housekeeper will find occasionally bits of dry bread accumulated. This is a good way to utilize them: Soak in warm water several hours before supper or breakfast, adding plenty of milk, if convenient. Mash up with a spoon when soft, adding 1 beaten egg, a cupful or more of flour, a teaspoon of soda, if needed, and a teaspoon of sugar. Bake same as buckwheats. They are very nice. No bread need be wasted, even if somewhat sodden, heavy, or a little sour.

SUNSHINE FRUIT

Add 1 lb. sugar to 1 lb. of fruit; to sugar add a little water; let boil till it threads. Drop the fruit in and boil 15 minutes; pour out on platter and set in sunshine for 6 hours. Put away in glasses; paraffin top. Especially good for strawberries.

VANILLA CREAM
1860

Boil a vanilla bean in a quart of rich milk until it has imparted the flavor sufficiently. Then take it out and mix with the milk, 8 eggs, yolks and whites beaten well. Let it boil a little longer. Make it very sweet, for much of the sugar is lost in the operation of freezing. When ice creams are not put into shapes, they should always be served in glasses with handles.

YEAST
1850 — Nancy Leanorah Matthews

Put ½ tbsp. of pressed hops, or a heaping handful of unpressed hops, into 3 qts. of water and boil gently half an hour. Strain off the liquor, and when milk warm, add half a pint of brown sugar and 2 tbsp. of salt. With a little of this hop-water, wet 1 lb. of

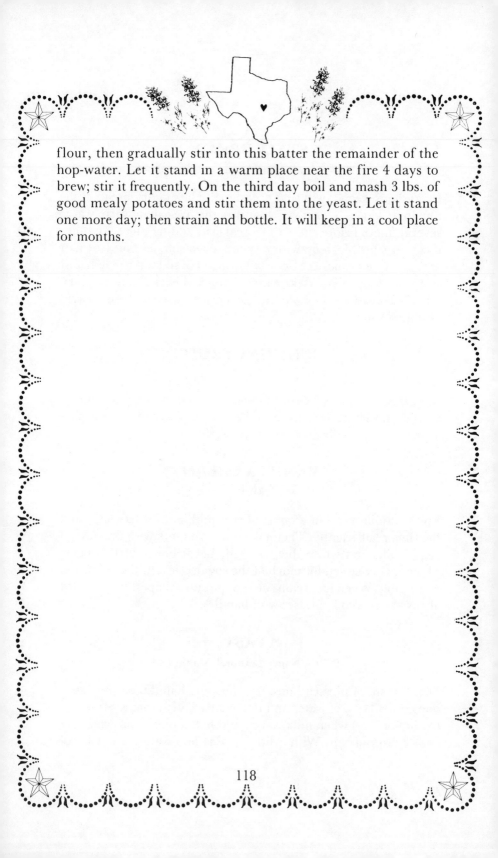

flour, then gradually stir into this batter the remainder of the hop-water. Let it stand in a warm place near the fire 4 days to brew; stir it frequently. On the third day boil and mash 3 lbs. of good mealy potatoes and stir them into the yeast. Let it stand one more day; then strain and bottle. It will keep in a cool place for months.

Household Hints

Creeping Things

ANT TRAP

1820 — Delilah Smith Brown

Procure a large sponge, wash it well and press it dry, which will leave the cells quite open; then sprinkle over it some fine white sugar and place it near where the ants are most troublesome. They will soon collect upon the sponge and take up their abode in the cells. Dip sponge in scalding water. Repeat process and place in new spot.

BEDBUGS

1840 — From Grandmother Matthews's Scrapbook

The only certain cure for bedbugs is a solution of corrosive sublimate, which may be obtained at the druggist's. The bedsteads should be taken apart and well washed with cold water and hand soap; then with a small flat brush the poison should be applied to every crack and crevice where a bug may harbor. The poison should be used once or twice a week, as may be necessary. It is a work of time and patience, but if persevered in this remedy will effectually destroy the bugs. Corrosive sublimate is a deadly poison and should be kept out of the way of children and servants.

BLUE BUGS IN THE HEN HOUSE
1895 — Emmett Barnett

Blue bugs were a sort of tick that would attach themselves to poultry and suck the blood until the bird died. They reproduced rapidly and when they invaded the hen house, they could wipe out an entire flock in a very short time.

My daddy, Emmett Barnett, would ask our merchant at the general store to save him the banana stalk when the bananas were all sold. He placed this banana stalk in the hen house, and the blue bugs were soon all gone.

HEAD LICE, CHINCHES, AND BEDBUGS

For head lice, shingle hair close and use kerosene. For chinches or bedbugs, burn sulfur in a closed house.

INSECTICIDE
1850

Hot alum water is the best insect destroyer known. Put the alum in hot water and let it boil till it is all dissolved; then apply the solution hot with a brush to all cracks, closets, bedsteads, and other places, where any insects are found. Ants, bedbugs, cockroaches, and creeping things are killed by it, while it has no danger of poisoning the family or injuring the property.

PROTECTION AGAINST MOTHS
1800 — Wilhelmina Kuhn Palm

Closets that have moths should be well rubbed with a decoction of tobacco and repeatedly sprinkled with spirits of camphor. Pieces of paper soaked with the same are good.

[Wilhelmina Kuhn Palm came to Texas in 1846 on the ship Orient *from Germany and settled at Cat Springs, Texas.]*

Apparel / Sewing

CALICO PRINTING
1865

This art consists in dyeing cloth with certain colors and figures upon a ground of a different hue; the colors, when they will not take hold of cloth readily, are fixed to them by means of mordants, as a preparation of alum, made by dissolving 3 lbs. of alum and 1 lb. of acetate of lead in 8 lbs. of warm water. There are added at the same time 2 oz. of potash and 2 oz. of chalk. Acetate of iron also is a mordant in frequent use in the printing of calicos, but the simple mixture of alum and acetate of lead is found to answer best as a mordant.

FADING COLORS

To prevent colors fading, dip new fabrics in salt water.

HEARTH RUGS
1850 — Nancy Leanorah Matthews

First, procure a piece of coffee sack. Make it the size you wish. From old half-worn pants and flannel skirts tear strips about 1½ inches wide. Then begin in the center with one long strip (or if you prefer, a large square piece) and sew a strip of old pants around the center strip. Alternate with the flannel skirts torn in strips the same width, and put on as you make a log cabin quilt. When nicely bound, you will have a rug which for use and economy cannot be excelled.

HOMEMADE DYES
1899 — Edna Barnett

Brown — for a beautiful warm brown, boil walnut hulls and use the water to dye the domestic.

Yellow — made from boiling agarita roots.

Purple — crush the berries from poke salad. Simmer and strain.

121

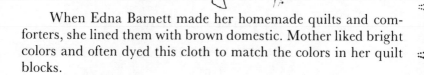

When Edna Barnett made her homemade quilts and comforters, she lined them with brown domestic. Mother liked bright colors and often dyed this cloth to match the colors in her quilt blocks.

INFANTS' CLOTHES

Some females in dressing an infant are very rough and must harass and fatigue it much. The most tender deliberation should be observed. Never let the clothes be tight. Never use pins, for they are dangerous. The strings must be tied so slack that one might get two fingers between.

KNITTING
1850

If in taking off the stitches for the heel of a sock they would make it seven or eight stitches wider than usual and knit like a double mitten, only looser, and the toe the same way, they will have the best double heel and toe that can be made, and save a vast amount of darning.

NINE TOILETS MADE FROM THREE

Listen, and I will tell you how I can wear nine distinct toilets and really have but three. First, I have one cream white parasol and fan. These by changing the bow on the parasol and the ribbon on the fan, go with any toilet. Secondly, I have three light dresses — a white pique, a pink French bunting, and a blue lawn. Then I have three sets of ribbons — that is a whole set consisting of parasol bow, sash, ribbons, fan ribbon, slipper bow, and hair bow. Then I have a pink set of ribbons and a blue set. My pink and blue are light, so I can wear my three dresses with ribbons to match, or I can cross them. I can put a light pink sash on a light blue dress or a light blue sash on a light pink dress. Then you can see that with three dresses and three sets of ribbons I can make nine distinct toilets.

SCIENTIFIC PATCHING

Nancy Leanorah Matthews

I shall begin with the perhaps original axiom that a patch must be rectangular. A round or a "crooked" one will inevitably thrust itself into notice, as it is impossible to match the threads. Then a patch should never be laid on, but always set in. To this end, first cut away carefully by a thread all that is in the least worn, and turn back and baste down an even seam all around. The corners may be slashed slightly in a diagonal direction to keep them square. Then to this opening fit the patch exactly with the edges turned and basted; and sew it in "over and over" on the wrong side with thread of the precise shade and very fine, sewing alternate opposite sides to avoid trouble with the corners. The extra thickness caused by the folded corners of the patch itself should be cut out after sewing, and a little fine darning added to keep them secure. Now slightly dampen and press on the wrong side, and you have a neat piece of mending which cannot be seen a few feet away.

[Nancy Leanorah Carothers Matthews lived in the Liberty Hill area about 1853 when she was a young girl. She walked three miles to school in the summer because in the winter she was busy spinning, weaving, and making clothes. Wool was clipped from the sheep, corded, and made into thread on the spinning wheel. It was then woven into cloth on the loom. Then, patterns and clothes were made. No doubt she excelled in "Scientific Patching" and she left her instructions behind in a scrapbook.]

STRETCHING SHOES

Fill shoes with cottonseeds that have been soaked in water. Pack tightly, then lace shoes up. *Caution:* Shoes will sometimes bust open when seeds dry.

TIPS FOR THE STOUT WOMAN

1870

Avoid dainty and spindly chairs and furniture which serve to accentuate your bigness. Hats with wide and slanting brims are usually best. Wear gloves which match the sleeves in color.

Avoid shoes with heels too high. Slender and dark-colored shoes are usually better than light ones. Use fine-textured stockings as dark as the current fashion allows. Use a medium-sized hand-bag, preferably square or rectangular. Too small a bag empha-sizes your stoutness and too large a bag may look too bulky. If you carry an umbrella use a long, slender one.

Cleaning

CLEANING A BLACK CALICO DRESS AND HOW TO KEEP IT FROM FADING

On a nice, clear day make a warm, hardwater suds and wash the dress out in it, but do not put on any soap; the soap in the water will be sufficient. Then rinse in hard, boiling water. Make a thin starch, boil it well, and starch on the wrong side. Hang it up where it will dry as quickly as possible, and it will not be faded a bit. This is a good way to wash the polka dot cambrics and cali-cos so fashionable now.

CLEANING BLACK FROM POTS
1859 — Lei Red Purcell

Take ashes from fireplace and use corn cob dipped in water. Rub until all black is removed from the bottom of the pot.

CLEANING WITH NEWSPAPER
1860

Save the old paper — never throw away old paper. If you have no wish to sell it, use it in the house. Some housekeepers prefer it to cloth for cleaning many articles of furniture. For instance, a volume written by a lady who prided herself on her experience and tact, says: "After the stove has been blackened, it can be kept looking very well for a long time by rubbing it with paper every morning." Rubbing with paper is a much nicer way of keeping the outside of a tea kettle, coffeepot, or teapot bright and clean than the old way of washing them in suds. Rubbing with paper is also the best way of polishing knives, tinware, and spoons; they shine like new silver. For polishing mirrors, windows, lamp chimneys, etc., paper is better than dry cloth. Preserves and pickles keep much better if brown paper, instead of cloth, is tied over the jar. Canned fruit is not so apt to mold if a piece of writing paper, cut to fit the can, is laid directly on the fruit. Paper is much better to put under a carpet than straw. It is warmer, thinner, and makes less noise when one walks over it.

CLEANING CHILDREN'S HEADS

Take half a pint of wheat bran in a tin dish, turn a quart of boiling water upon it, stir it thoroughly, and let it stand and settle till cold. Drain off the liquor and add a teaspoonful of spirits of ammonia.

CLEANING GREASE FROM STOVE
1890

If you spill grease on a hot stove, cover with a thick layer of ashes; this will absorb the grease so you will not be offended by the odor as it burns. Later brush away the ashes and none of the grease will remain.

CLEANING THE STOVE
1850 — Grandmother Matthews's Scrapbook

I have known persons to spend two hours in blackening a stove, and be so tired after it that nothing more could be accomplished that day. This is a useless waste of time and strength. Here is the best way to do it. Have your stove perfectly cold, and, if possible, in a room with the windows open, as the air assists the progress greatly. Apply the stove polish with an old brush to a portion of your stove and rub over with your polishing brush for a minute or two; then leave it to dry a little while you serve another portion in the same manner. But be careful that it does not dry too much, or it will be gray in spite of all you can do. Then return to it and polish briskly for several minutes. In this manner go over the whole stove, returning to the charge again and again, until the brightness begins to appear, at first grayish-black, but becoming as the friction is continued a rich jet black, both durable and beautiful.

This is for the castings. For the sheetiron parts as well as for the stovepipes, use a soft flannel cloth to apply the blacking, a small portion at a time, and rub up instantly with another flannel cloth, and in a few minutes you will have a smooth, polished surface in which you may see your own grimy countenance reflected.

CLEANING OSTRICH FEATHERS
1870

White or light-tinted ones can be laid on a plate and scrubbed gently with a toothbrush, in warm soapy suds, then well shaken out and well dried, whether by the hot sun or a good fire. At first the feather will have a most discouraging appearance, and a novice is apt to think it perfectly spoiled. But after it is dry it should be carefully curled with a pen knife or scissors blade, and it will recover all its former plumy softness.

DUSTCLOTHS
1872 — Nettie Reid McCarty

When soiled, wash in warm soapsuds. Rinse thoroughly in clear, lukewarm water. Dry. Dip in lemon oil solution. Re-dry. Store in tightly covered metal box.

TREATED DUSTERS
1872 — Nettie Reid McCarty

Combine 1 pint hot water and 1/4 cup lemon oil. Dip 4 or 5 squares (20″ x 20″) in solution. Press solution through cloth thoroughly. Squeeze out all excess moisture. Dry thoroughly.

Flowers

BEAUTIFY HOME

Flowers are suggestive of many very pretty and beautiful thoughts, and no one who is fond of flowers can really be bad at heart; for a love of flowers is sure to spring from a mind which admires the beautiful in nature with a fervor which is no mere passing fancy. No home is worthy of the name which does not possess a few choice flowers, either indoors or out, and a place looks barren indeed without them. They add greatly to the appearance of the surroundings, and give that air of grace and refinement which nothing else can. The very many arduous duties which necessarily devolve upon farmers' wives and daughters should not prevent them from bestowing a few spare moments each day in caring for a neatly kept bed of flowers in the yard. We have heard some say that if deprived of this pleasure they would soon become morose and weary of the never-ceasing routine of household duties which it is theirs to perform. We do not advise planting or keeping many flowers, for the care of them will either become a real burden or else they will get neglected. Beautify your home and you will thus make it more attractive for the younger members of your family as well as for yourself.

BOUQUETS

The flowers should not be crowded, as each kind has its individuality. Put scarlet, crimson, and purple in separate bunches and use white to blend them. Yellow should be used sparingly; too much will produce a glare. Ferns help in giving lightness and relief to a bouquet.

FERTILIZER
1850

Liquid manure for flowers can be made by taking one bushel of the clippings from horses' hoofs and put in a barrel. Fill with water. Let it stand for a week, when it is ready for use.

SWEETENED POTS

A few drops of ammonia added to a gallon of water and applied once a week to all pots of flowers will do much good and keep the pots and earth from souring.

Furniture and Floors

FURNITURE POLISH

1861 — Mary E. Sprinkle Vaughn

Mix equal parts sweet oil, lemon juice, and cornstarch.

OIL FLOORS

Take one gallon of linseed oil and add burnt lube, about a pound. Mix well and wipe on floor with wool rag.

PAINT FOR FLOORS

There is but one paint suitable for floors, and that is French ochre. First, if the boards have shrunk, clean out the joints well, and with a small brush give a heavy coat of boiled linseed oil; then putty up solid. Now paint the whole floor with a mixture of much oil and little ochre for the first coat; after it is well dried, give two more coats of much ochre and little oil; finally, finish with a coat of first-rate copal varnish.

PAINT AND VARNISH REMOVER

Cook until thick: 2 cups water and 2 teaspoons cornstarch; remove from heat. Best to take outside to add ½ cup washing soda and ½ cup ammonia. Paint on furniture every 15 minutes for 3 times. Wash off with hot water and suds.

Grooming

CHAPPED HANDS

1845 — Caroline Virginia Rogers Carroll

Scrape beeswax lightly into a small, wide-mouthed bottle until it is nearly full; add a small piece of mutton tallow and fill with olive oil. Set the bottle on the back of the stove, and as soon as

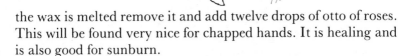

the wax is melted remove it and add twelve drops of otto of roses. This will be found very nice for chapped hands. It is healing and is also good for sunburn.

[Caroline Carroll came to Texas in 1888 with her husband and only daughter, Martha.]

COLOGNE
1886 — Nancy Elizabeth Standifer Davis

Cologne alcohol, 1 pt.; oils of English lavender and bergamot, each 1½ drops; oil of rosemary, ½ drop; oil of cinnamon, 2 drops; essence of lemon, 1½ drops. Mix.

COMPLEXION
1850 — Hannah Elizabeth Hall Denny

½ pt. of new milk, ½ oz. of white brandy, ¼ oz. of lemon juice, boiled together. Skim clean from scum, and use night and morning. It will remove tan and freckles caused by the sun and wind.

FACE POWDER

Take of wheat starch, 1 lb.; powdered orris-root, 3 oz.; oil of lemon, 30 drops; oil of bergamot, oil of cloves, each 15 drops. Rub thoroughly together.

FRECKLES CURE

Take beef's gall, ½ oz.; saleratus, borax, and gum grarac, of each ¼ oz. (pulverized); alcohol and rosewater, of each ¼ pt.; mix and let stand 10 days, shaking occasionally. Use as a wash twice a day. You can get this wash made up at the drug stores; it will cost you about 30 cents.

CLEANING THE HAIR
1840 — Elisabetha Margaretha Volk

Take 1 oz. of borax and ½ oz. of camphor. Powder these ingredients fine, and dissolve in 1 qt. of boiling water. When cold, the solution will be ready for use. Dampen the hair with this fre-

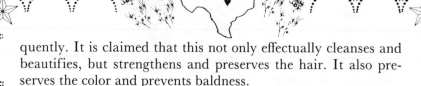

quently. It is claimed that this not only effectually cleanses and beautifies, but strengthens and preserves the hair. It also preserves the color and prevents baldness.

[Elisabetha came to the Port Lavaca area in early 1828.]

DANDRUFF
1900

Take an ounce of sulphur and a quart of water; shake every few hours and saturate the head every morning with the liquid. The dandruff will disappear in a week or so, and the hair will become bright and glossy.

GREY HAIR PREVENTION
1819 — Elisabetha Margaretha Volk

The hair should be well brushed every day, and be wet at the roots with strong sage tea — one ounce of borax to every quart of the tea. Wet the scalp, and then brush for fully ten minutes. This will make harsh, rough hair become smooth and glossy.

GREY HAIR RECIPE

To $1/2$ pt. of water add 1 oz. of bay rum, a small box barbo compound, and $1/4$ oz. of glycerine. Apply to the hair twice a week until the desired shade you want. Any druggist can mix it or you can do it yourself at home at very little cost. Full directions come in each box of barbo compound. It will darken streaked and faded grey hair and remove dandruff. It is excellent for falling hair and will make harsh hair soft and glossy.

HAIR CURLING
1850

Oil to make the hair curl: Use olive oil, 1 lb.; oil of organum, 1 drachma; oil of rosemary, $1^1/2$ drachmas.

HAIR INVIGORATOR
1892 — Dorothea Schluens Palm

Bay rum, 2 pts.; alcohol, 1 pt.; castor oil, 1 oz.; carbonated ammonia, 1/2 oz.; tincture of cantharides, 1 oz. Mix them well. This compound will promote the growth of the hair and prevent it from falling out.

[Dorothea came with her family to Texas in 1847.]

HAND LOTION

This recipe was handed down from her mother to my mother-in-law, Lilly Varan. Made up in a quantity four times larger than the recipe given, this mixture was kept by the washbowl and was used frequently and generously each time her hands were washed. Lilly, who died in 1986, had the softest, whitest hands one has ever seen on an octagenarian.

4 oz. rubbing alcohol   1/2 ox. glycerine
4 oz. rosewater   1/8 oz. benzoin
2 oz. peroxide

☆   ☆   ☆

RECIPE FOR QUARRELING

Take a root of sassafras and steep in a pint of water and put in a bottle and when your husband comes in to quarrel fill your mouth with it and hold until he goes away. A sure cure.

SOFT SKIN CARE
1850 — Asa Wright and John Lloyd Halliburton families

Keep a covered dish of oatmeal on your washstand instead of soap. Take a handful of meal; moisten and rub the hands thoroughly with it. This will whiten and soften the skin.

SOFT SKIN OINTMENT
1865

Take of olive oil, 5 oz.; white wax, 1 oz. This is a useful emollient ointment for softening the skin.

BEAUTIFUL TEETH
1850 — Emily Barnhill Houston

Dissolve in 3 pts. of boiling water 2 oz. of borax. Add 1 tsp. of spirits of camphor. When you take a glass of water to brush your teeth, pour in a little. It is very pleasant and will strengthen the gums.

BLACK TEETH
1850 — Emily Barnhill Houston

Pulverize equal parts of salt and cream of tartar, and mix them thoroughly. After washing the teeth in the morning, rub them with this powder. After a few applications the blackness will disappear.

[Emily was the wife of Andrew Deavers Houston, who was a first cousin to Sam Houston.]

CARE OF THE TEETH
1864 — Susannah Dickinson

Never allow a particle of food to remain between the teeth. Use the brush before breakfast and after each meal. Brush the back of the teeth as well as the front. Pure castile soap is better than powder. Use a toothpick freely after each meal.

[Susannah was a survivor of the fall of the Alamo. Released by General Santa Anna, Susannah was sent to Gonzales on a pony to deliver a letter written by Santa Anna to citizens of that town. She brought the news of the fall of the Alamo.]

CLEANING THE TEETH
1840 — Nancy Leanorah Matthews

A good way to clean teeth is to dip the brush in water, rub it over genuine white castile soap, then dip it in prepared chalk. I have been complimented upon the whiteness of my teeth, which were originally anything but white. I have used the soap constantly

for two or three years, and the chalk for the last year. There is no danger of scratching the teeth, as the chalk is prepared. With a good stiff brush and the soap, this is as effectual as soap and sand on a floor.

TOOTH POWDER AND BRUSH
1859 — Lel Red Purcell

Make a mixture of salt and soda. Brush teeth at least after each meal. When need to whiten teeth, add lemon juice to mixture on brush. The best brush is made from hackberry or peach limb. Take a small limb, skin the bark back, about $1/2$ inch, and chew the end there. Spread the parts and use on teeth. About $1/4$ inch limb is best. Also can use fig root.

[Grandmother Purcell never used a toothbrush except when she went visiting. Her father was an early pioneer doctor, and he gave her this method.]

PERSPIRATION

The unpleasant odor produced by perspiration is frequently the source of vexation to persons who are subject to it. Nothing is simpler than to remove this odor much more effectually than by the application of such costly unguents and perfumes as are in use. It is only necessary to procure some of the compound spirits of ammonia, and place about two tablespoonfuls in a basin of water. Washing the face, hands, and arms with this leaves the skin as clean, sweet, and fresh as one could wish. The wash is perfectly harmless and very cheap.

SUNBURNS AND WRINKLES
1860

Milk of almonds, obtained at the druggist's, is as good as anything to use. To keep wrinkles out of the face, use tepid water instead of cold; if the wrinkles are deep-seated, apply a little turpentine to the wrinkles for a few nights before retiring. Some

ladies use a patch of court plaster for the wrinkles, which soon eradicates these emblems of care and age.

WRINKLES IN THE SKIN

White wax, 1 oz.; strained honey, 2 oz.; juice of lily-bulbs, 2 oz. The foregoing melted and stirred together will remove wrinkles.

Home Hints

LAMP WICKS
1883 — Ada Lowell Wilson Baldeschwiler

Soak lamp wicks in vinegar and they will not smoke.

PRESSED LEAVES
1860

A good way to arrange autumn leaves and ferns is to stitch or pin or iron them on with thin mucilage to a strip of lace of suitable width, and with it border lace or muslin curtains and lambrequins. This confines them so they will not easily be broken, and the light falling through brings out the colors finely and the whole produces a charming effect. A room can be ornamented by twisting the stems of autumn leaves on the wire as milliners do artificial flowers, twining the sprays about walls, windows, and pictures, like vines.

ROCK GARDEN INDOORS
Written in back of Grandmother Raven's cookbook, original source and time frame unknown.

Place a coal cinder, any size desired, in a glass dish. Take 2 tbsp. of bluing and 4 tbsp. of salt, sprinkle over the coal, and wet with 4 tbsp. of water. Every other morning just dampen the coal with water and sprinkle a tiny pinch of salt over it. In about two weeks you will have a fairy garden.

Kitchen Hints

AROMA OF BUTTER
1860

The milk, as soon as it is drawn, and while yet warm, is filtered through a sprig of washed fir tips, the stem of which is inserted loose and upright in the hole of the funnel. The milk deposits any hair, skins, clots, or gelatinous sliminess it may contain on the clear, spicular leaves. It has imparted to it a most agreeable odor and does not readily sour. A fresh sprig should be used each time.

CLEANING FLATWARE
1880

It is not generally known that for scouring knives, forks, spoons, and tinware, the common water lime such as is used in plastering cisterns, cellars, etc. is one of the very best materials. It does not scratch and will not injure your best silver. Apply with a damp cloth. The more often such things are cleansed, the more easily they are cleaned.

DEODORIZER

Coffee roasted, ground, and exposed in an open vessel is a more powerful deodorizer than chloride of lime, without its disagreeable smell.

DRESSING CHICKENS
1883 — Ada Lowell Wilson Baldeschwiler

When dressing chickens, add one tablespoon soda to the water in which they are scalded and the pin feathers will come out much easier.

GREASE REMOVAL

Put on powder of French chalk and place a piece of blotting paper over it; then pass a hot iron over the blotting paper. The heat liquifies the grease, the chalk absorbs it, and the excess of grease is absorbed by the blotting paper.

ICE WATER

To make water almost as cold as ice, without the use of ice: Let the jar, pitcher, or vessel used for water be surrounded with one or more folds of coarse cotton kept constantly wet. The evaporation of the water will carry off the heat from the inside, and reduce it to a freezing point.

OLD BACON
1830

For those who are not convenient to a market house, old bacon is much improved by putting it in a batter of milk and flour before frying.

SILVER TARNISH

Silver will not tarnish if a piece of alum is placed in the drawer with the silverware.

SPATTERING LARD

To keep lard from spattering while frying, sprinkle in a little salt.

SWEET MILK PRESERVATION

A spoonful of grated horseradish in the pan will keep it for several days.

VEGETABLE HINTS

Top-of-the-ground vegetables should be cooked in salted water. Underground vegetables should be salted after cooking.

WASHING OILCLOTH

Wash oilcloths with salt water, say, one pint salt dissolved in a pailful of water. When dry, wipe over with a little milk and water. Sweep oilcloth well. Wash with cold water, using a brush. Then wash with milk and wipe dry. Never use hot water.

WILTED VEGETABLES
Grandmother Raven's Cookbook

If your vegetables become wilted and stale before you can use them, place them for an hour or so in a gallon of water to which a teaspoon of soda has been added. They will be as fresh and crisp as when gathered from the garden.

Washing

BLEACHING CLOTHES
1860

Use kerosene to bleach clothes by putting a cupful of kerosene into wash boiler of soapy water before fire is lighted to boil water.

BLUING (LIQUID)
1900

Most of the bluing sold is poor stuff, leaving specks in the clothes. To avoid this: Take best Prussian-blue, pulverized, 1 oz.; oxalle acid, also pulverized, 1/2 oz.; soft water, 1 qt. Mix. The acid dissolves the blue and holds it evenly in the water, so that specking will never take place. One or two tablespoons of it is sufficient for a tub of water, according to the size of the tub.

CLEARING WATER
Grandmother Raven's Cookbook

When washing water is muddy, fill a large barrel full of water and into it put a gallon of ashes; let set about four hours, when water will be clear.

WASHDAY

The clothes are examined, and those which are least soiled are first put in a tub of warm water. I do not advocate soaking them. It may make them wash easier, but it gives them a grayish look. These are soaped and thoroughly rubbed, thrown into a second tub, turned, soaped, and rubbed again. They are now ready to place in a boiler of cold water, to which you may add soap or not, and boiled. When they begin to boil, dip into a tub of cold water. Wring with a wringer and throw into a tub of well water, which has been slightly hued with indigo. Here they may stay as long as you please. The coarse clothes go through the same process, being kept separate from first to last.

After the fine clothes have been removed from the boiler, dip out enough hot water to admit cold water poured in sufficient to render it lukewarm. Proceed as before. Towels and table-cloths must be boiled by themselves. The rubbing suds has done its duty, and for it we have no further use. The water into which the boiled clothes were put, with that left in the boiler, will answer for colored garments, which must not be allowed to lie in water any longer than necessary, but should be turned, starched, and hung in the shade to dry to prevent fading. In hanging the clothes on the line, do not hang half on one side and half on the other, but as near singly as possible; both for the sake of appearance and bleaching. I have washed in this way for many years and very frequently have the pleasure of hearing "how white your washing looks."

Usually, the clothes are left on the line till the dew falls. The unstarched then need no dampening but are folded in the basket as taken from the line. Do not break or bend starched garments. Handle carefully. Sprinkle well. Roll tightly and place with the others, putting a towel between white and colored clothes. Black and white goods look better if ironed immediately after sprinkling.

IRONING CLOTHES
1883 — Ada Lowell Wilson Baldeschwiler

Put a little white soap in starch to make clothes easier to iron.

IRONING HAT VEILS
1880

Hat veils may be ironed by placing between sheets of waxed paper.

HOMEMADE LYE SOAP
1836 — Asa Wright and John Lloyd Halliburton families

Put 2 gallons of water in an old black iron washpot and build a fire around the pot. When the fire burns down and the water is hot, add 3 cans of lye, stirring well with a wooden paddle until lye is dissolved. Add 15 lbs. of grease, meat rinds, etc. and cook until lye has dissolved all grease and pork rinds, stirring continuously. When all grease and rinds are dissolved, add 1 qt. of water, cook and stir another 20 minutes. Set pot away from fire and stir until soap is thick. Let cool. The next day it will be ready to cut in chunks and store in a cool, dry place. The longer the soap sits, the better it is.

INEXPENSIVE HOMEMADE SOAP
1868 — Mrs. Joe Lela Duty Nash

This soap can easily be made at home and five or six pounds can be made in half an hour. I use five pounds of beef drippings, one can of lye (10¢), one-half pound of borax (5¢), and one-half cupful of ammonia (about 3¢). Take the lye and dilute it with six cupfuls of cold water; then add the borax and ammonia. After it is fully dissolved, have the fat melted but not hot and mix the two together, stirring the mixture with a long stick for eight minutes. It should be as thick as honey. Have in readiness wooden or pasteboard boxes (corset boxes are excellent for the purpose)

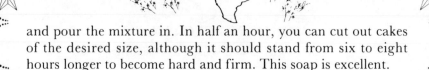

and pour the mixture in. In half an hour, you can cut out cakes of the desired size, although it should stand from six to eight hours longer to become hard and firm. This soap is excellent.

ONE HUNDRED POUNDS OF GOOD SOAP FOR $1.80
1900

Take potash, 6 lbs. (75 cts.); lard, 4 lbs. (50 cts.); resin, ¼ lb. (5 cts.). Beat up the resin, mix all together, and set aside for 5 days; then put the whole into a 10-gallon cask of warm water, and stir twice a day for 10 days; at the expiration of which time you will have one hundred pounds of excellent soap.

STARCH FOR COLLARS
1860 — Nancy Leanorah Matthews

Mix very gradually one tablespoon of white starch with half a pint of cold water. Dissolve a small piece of borax in hot water; when cold, stir it into the starch. Put the collars in, rub them up and down in it, and press them in a cloth. Iron immediately: press with a flat iron, then with a polishing iron.

STARCH POLISH FOR LINENS
1860

Take of white wax, one ounce, spermaceti, two ounces, and a good pinch of salt. Mix and melt them together, and when cold it will be a hard, white cake that will not mold or sour even in hot weather. Put a piece the size of a pea in the hot starch that is sufficient for three or four shirts. When ironing, go over them a second time quickly, which increases the gloss or polish. The best kind of a polishing iron is the one with a bulge at both ends — a kind that costs a dollar at the hardware store. Iron it well once; then dampen with a perfectly clean, soft, white moist cloth. Then rub with the polishing iron until it is so glossy you can see your face in it. The iron must not be too hot or it will scorch; if it is a little too cool, the polish will be longer coming.

WASHING FLUID
1900

Saving Half the Wash-Board Labor: Salt soda, 1 lb.; stone lime, 1/2 lb.; water, 5 qts. Boil a short time, stirring occasionally; then let it settle and pour off the clear fluid into a stone jug, and cork for use. Soak your white clothes overnight, in simple water; wring out, and soap wristbands, collars, and dirty or stained places. Have your boiler half-filled with water, and when at scalding heat, put in one common teacup of the fluid, stir, and put in your clothes. Boil for half an hour; then rub lightly through one suds only, rinsing well in the bluing water, as usual, and all is complete. If you wish to wash on Monday, put warm suds to the clothes whilst breakfast is being got ready; then wring out and soap as above. Will do just as well as soaking them overnight, and my wife thinks better.

Miscellaneous

CEDAR TREES
1898 — Velma Price Hall

Have you ever wondered why, at old pioneer home sites in Texas, there is always a cedar tree planted near the front door? Our ancestors used cedar for many things. Here are a few listed:

1. Makes ironing easier by using wax from running a hot flat iron over a sprig of cedar.
2. Lay fans of cedar between clothes stored in wardrobes and drawers to repel insects and freshen clothes.
3. Used as air freshener for damp houses.
4. Decorations for Christmas seasons.
5. Use cedar fans to cool yourself and switch away insects while sitting on the porch.
6. Also used for medicinal purposes.

DRIVING NAILS

Nails and screws dipped in soap will drive more easily into hard wood.

FOUL AIR

The quickest way to expel foul air from a well is to heat a bar of iron red-hot and lower it down into the water. The sudden formation of steam is effectual.

LEATHER LUSTRE

To revive the lustre of leather, apply the white of an egg with a sponge.

LIBRARY PASTE

1½ cups hot water   1 cup flour
½ cup sugar

Boil thick and add 5 drops oil of cloves, a good pinch of alum.

PLASTER OF PARIS

Plaster of Paris mixed with water to the consistency of cream forms an excellent article for mending lamps that have become loose, for covering cracks and holes in white walls, etc.

SKUNK ODORS

To kill skunk odors, mix vinegar and tomato juice in equal parts and rub on affected area.

TO ECONOMIZE THE SUNFLOWER
1865

The cultivation of the annual sunflower is recommended to the notice of the public, possessing the advantage of furnishing abundance of agreeable fodder for cattle in their leaves. When in flower, bees flock from all quarters to gather honey. The seed is valuable in feeding sheep, pigs, and other animals; it produces a striking effect in poultry, as occasioning them to lay more eggs, and it yields a large quantity of excellent oil by pressure. The dry

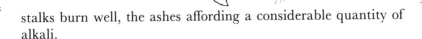

stalks burn well, the ashes affording a considerable quantity of alkali.

TO TOUGHEN NIPPLES FOR NURSING
1885 — Handed down from Michel family

Mix tannin and glycerine and apply during last month of pregnancy.

CHAPPED NIPPLES

Mix and dissolve baking soda and glycerine and apply to nipples and wash off before nursing.

Amusements for the Young

BLIND MAN'S BLUFF
1900

Choose which shall be the blind man, and then tie a handkerchief carefully over his eyes. Stand him in the middle of the room. Then one says to him: "How many cows has your father got?" He answers, "Three." "What color are they?" "Black, white, and gray." "Then turn around three times, and catch you may." The game then is to avoid being caught by the blind man. A good deal of fun is made by touching him on the back, arms, legs, and so on. As soon as one is caught, then that one becomes the blind man. This game can also be played in the gardens or fields.

KISS IN THE RING
1900

Join hands in a ring, a lady and a gentleman alternately; then, the one who is selected to begin the game stands in the middle, and the rest dance round and round, singing:

143

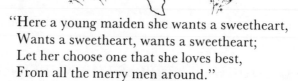

"Here a young maiden she wants a sweetheart,
Wants a sweetheart, wants a sweetheart;
Let her choose one that she loves best,
From all the merry men around."

It is usual to provide the lady with a handkerchief, which she throws at the feet of a young gentleman, who instantly picks it up and pursues her in and out the circle till he catches her. As soon as he has caught her he brings her into the ring, and the players again dance round and round, singing:

"Here's a couple both married together,
Like father and mother they must agree;
Love one another like sister and brother,
So pray, young couples, come kiss together."

The gentleman then salutes the lady, who joins the ring, leaving the gentleman in the middle. The game goes on as before, only substituting the words "man" for "maiden" and "maids" for "men." This is a merry garden game in the summertime, when the young gentlemen are not too rough.

DISCLAIMER

The home remedies and household hints contained in this book are provided for historical purposes only. No express or implied warranties with regard to their efficacy or safety are made by Daughters of the Republic of Texas, District VIII. Do not use them without first consulting a physician or other appropriate medical professional. Daughters of the Republic of Texas are not engaged in rendering medical advice.

Home Remedies

ASTHMA

1 pt. medicated linseed oil, 1 pt. honey, 1 pt. whiskey. Mix and take 1 tsp. three times a day.

BAD BREATH

1892 — Mattie Carroll Umland

Bad breath from catarrh, foul stomach, or bad teeth may be temporarily relieved by diluting a little bromo chloralum with 8 or 10 parts of water, and using it as a gargle, and swallowing a few drops before going out. A pint of bromo chloralum costs 50 cents, but a small vial will last a long time.

[Mattie Carroll came to Texas in 1888 to somewhere near Waller.]

BALDNESS

1900

Rub the part morning and evening with onions, till it is red, and afterwards with honey; or, wash it with a decoction of boxwood; or, electrify it daily. Or infuse for a few days, 1 dr. of powdered cantharides in 1 oz. of proof spirit; beef marrow, 1/2 lb.; soak in several waters, lastly in weak salt and water; melt, strain, and mix adding 10 or 12 drops of oil of bergamot, or lavender.

145

BLEEDING

Apply wet tea leaves or scrapings of sole-leather to a fresh cut or apply a paste of flour and vinegar. To stop bleeding from the nose, bathe the feet in very hot water, drinking at the same time a pint of cayenne pepper tea or hold both arms over the head.

★   ★   ★

Place a spider web across the wound.

★   ★   ★

Apply lamp black directly to the wound.

BLOOD BUILDERS

Take the young leaves of the poke plant, parboil them, season, fry, and then eat several messes.

BLOOD POISONING
1895

Mix equal parts of quinine and soda; spread on thin cloth and apply to affected parts. When cloth becomes green, remove and apply new one.

BLOOD PURIFIER
1900

Cut up and boil sassafras root to make tea. Flavor with sugar. Use to improve taste of other medicines, or drink to induce sweating. Use also as a spring tonic. The bark can be peeled from the root and boiled instead of the pulp.

BOILS OR INFECTIONS

Ingredients for making the salve: One part hog lard (pure lard at the store). Two parts of quinine (from drug store). (Example: Use 1 tsp. hog lard to 2 tsp. quinine.) To spread the salve easily, use more pure lard if needed.

To make the poultice: Sterilize with a hot iron a square cut from an

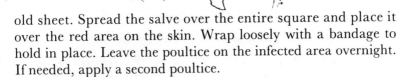

old sheet. Spread the salve over the entire square and place it over the red area on the skin. Wrap loosely with a bandage to hold in place. Leave the poultice on the infected area overnight. If needed, apply a second poultice.

In 1900, Dr. Hooe, a practicing country doctor who lived at Rosanky, Texas, gave the prescription for treating boils to my grandmother. Because she was moving from Rosanky, and her children seemed to have boils so often, Dr. Hooe gave her his secret prescription. It has been used in our family since then and has been very effective.

BOILS

Put a piece of very fat bacon or salt pork on the boil. Strap or tie it down. This will draw the infection.

BURNS
1897

Equal parts lime water and linseed oil.

★   ★   ★

Use lard and flour.

★   ★   ★

Put axle grease on the burned area.

CAKED BREASTS
1865 — Mrs. Plowman

Make some fried batter cakes. Rub butter on the breasts; lay the warm batter cakes on the breasts. This will make the milk start flowing and relieve the pain.

[Mrs. Plowman was never formally trained for nursing but had a natural talent in that field. Several doctors in the Pilgrim community area, Gonzales County, called upon her for assistance for many years. Once she was called away from church to help perform an appendectomy. Another time she spent a week with a young mother who had a blood vessel that burst in her leg. The doctor dipped the blood out with his hands, using the kitchen table for the necessary surgery.]

147

CATARRH

In the back of Grandmother Raven's Cookbook

1 qt. alcohol, 29¢	1 oz. oil of lavender, 35¢
1 oz. oil of peppermint, 75¢	1 oz. oil of organmum, 50¢
1 oz. oil of sassafras, 25¢	1 oz. oil of cloves, 35¢
1 oz. oil of hemlock, 25¢	2 oz. chloroform, 25¢

Dilute and use as desired. $3.10.

CHILLS AND FEVERS
1900

Boil peach tree leaves to make tea for chills and fever; button willow roots boiled low for chills and fever.

SLIPPERY-ELM BARK TEA FOR COLDS
1900

Break the bark into bits, pour boiling water over it, cover and let it infuse until cold. Sweeten, ice, and take for summer disorders, or add lemon juice and drink for a bad cold.

ONION GRUEL FOR COLDS

Slice down a few onions and boil them in a pint of new milk, stir in a sprinkle of oatmeal and a very little salt, boil till the onions are quite tender, then sup rapidly and go to bed.

COLDS

Juice of 2 lemons in glass of hot water, sweetened, and soda sufficient to cause a fermentation. Drink immediately after stirring in the soda and take it before retiring.

★　　★　　★

Make a poultice of kerosene, turpentine, and pure lard (the latter prevents blistering). Use wool cloth soaked with the mixture. Place cheese-cloth on chest for protection, and then add the wool poultice.

Make an onion poultice by roasting an onion, then wrapping it in spun-wool rags and beating it so that the onion juice soaks the rags well. Apply these rags to chest.

COLIC

Tie an asafetida bag around a baby's neck for six months to keep away six-month colic.

★　★　★

Take a pinch of soda in a spoon of water.

COUGH
1900

Mix 3 parts warm water, 1 part honey, and 1 part apple cider vinegar. Sip.

★　★　★

Cover 1 lemon with water; boil slowly 10 minutes. Extract juice; put juice in ½ pint jar. Add 2 tbsp. (1 oz.) glycerine; stir well. Finish filling jar with honey; shake well before using. Take it as needed, as often as every 3 hours.

★　★　★

1 part honey; 1 part raw linseed oil; 1 part 100-proof whiskey. Take 1 tablespoon every 2 hours by putting in mouth and let trickle down throat.

★　★　★

Dissolve four sticks of horehound candy in a pint of whiskey and take a couple of spoonfuls a day. This is also good for TB.

COUGH CANDY
Grandmother Raven's Cookbook

Break 2 oz. slippery elm bark into small bits. Add 1 cup water and 2 oz. flaxseed and let soak, stirring a few times, for 1 to 2 hours. Add 3 cups brown sugar, put on stove, stir until the sugar

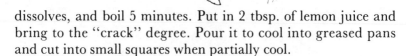

dissolves, and boil 5 minutes. Put in 2 tbsp. of lemon juice and bring to the "crack" degree. Pour it to cool into greased pans and cut into small squares when partially cool.

[This is a valuable remedy for those troubled with throat affections, or who use their voices much, and a pleasant candy as well.]

CROUP

For a baby, pour a mixture of turpentine and white whiskey into a saucer and set it afire. Hold the baby over the smoke until he breathes it deeply. This loosens him up.

KNIFE CUTS
1853

Clean wound well and apply a piece of fat bacon or fat back. Tie on or strap on for several days. Change if you need to do so.

PUNCTURE WOUNDS (NAILS, GUNSHOT)

Put some old wool rags into an old tin can, pour kerosene over the rags, and light. Then smoke the wound. This also works with chicken feathers.

KEROSENE TREATMENT

Pour kerosene oil over the cut, or soak it in same three times a day. This will also remove the soreness.

THORN POULTICE
1865

When anybody got mesquite thorns in their feet, Mama would make a poultice by taking the thorns and skin off of a prickly pear leaf. She would lay the leaf over the thorn and wrap a white rag all around it. By the next day, when we'd take it off, that old thorn would pop right out!

DIARRHEA CURE: BLACKBERRY BRANDY
1900

To half a gallon of blackberry juice put 1½ lbs. of lump sugar, ½ oz. of cinnamon, ½ oz. of grated nutmeg, ¼ oz. of cloves, and 1 oz. of allspice. Boil it a few minutes, and when cool, add 1 pt. of brandy. This is an invaluable remedy for diarrhea.

★ ★ ★

To stop diarrhea, place rice in pan, cover with water, bring to a boil, pour water off, and have the person drink this starchy water.

DIPHTHERIA REMEDY

Gargle the throat with a mixture of sulphur and water — 1 tsp. of sulphur to ½ teacupful of cold water. Swallow the gargle carefully, so as to make it penetrate every part of the throat.

DYSENTERY
1875

Drink a tea made of willow leaves or strawberry leaves.

EAR/REMOVAL OF OBJECTS
1840 — Nancy Leanorah Matthews

Take a horse-hair about six inches long and double it so as to make a loop at one end. Introduce this loop as deeply as possible into the auditory canal, and twist it gently around. After one or two turns, the foreign body is drawn out with the loop. The method is ingenious, and at all events causes little pain and can do no harm.

EARACHE
1850

Remedy never known to fail: Take a bit of cotton batting, put upon it a pinch of black pepper, gather it up and tie it, dip in sweet oil, and insert into the ear. Put a flannel bandage over the head to keep it warm. It will give instant relief.

EARACHE
1886

Take a large onion and cut into slices. Put a slice of onion, a slice of strong tobacco, a slice of onion, then tobacco. Wrap in a wet cloth and cover in hot embers, till onion is cooked. Press out the juice and drop into the ear. It gives instant relief — 3 or 4 drops of the juice at first.

EARACHE
1890

Pour castor oil, sweet oil, or machine oil into ear.

☆　　☆　　☆

EYES

To give brilliancy to the eyes, shut them early at night and open them early in the morning; let the mind be constantly intent on the acquisition of benevolent feelings. This will scarcely ever fail to impart to the eyes an intelligent and amiable expression.

☆　　☆　　☆

CINDER IN THE EYE
1880 — Grandmother Matthews

Persons traveling by railway are subject to continued annoyance from the flying cinders. On getting into the eye they are not only painful for the moment, but are often the cause of long suffering that ends in a total loss of sight. A very simple and effective cure is within the reach of everyone, and would prevent much suffering and expense were it more generally known. It is simply one or two grains of flaxseed. These may be placed in the eye without injury or pain to that delicate organ, and shortly they begin to swell and dissolve a glutinous substance that covers the ball of the eye, enveloping any foreign substance that may be in it. The irritation of cutting of the membrane is thus prevented, and the

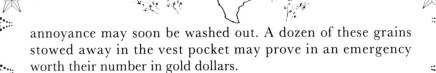

annoyance may soon be washed out. A dozen of these grains stowed away in the vest pocket may prove in an emergency worth their number in gold dollars.

STY ON THE EYE CURE

Cut a strip of brown paper sack 4 inches wide and 4 inches long. Wet with warm water. Place a small heap of salt in center of strip. Fold into a 2-inch square and tape over eye. It is best to do this just before going to bed at night and let it remain overnight.

FAINTING OR WEAKNESS
1853 — Laura Gayle Wilson

1 8-oz. cup rye whiskey, 1 small string (about 4 inches) rock candy. As much rock camphor as the liquid will take. It won't take too much, probably about 2 good tablespoons. Let the whole thing set for a week or two. It gets stronger as it sets.

FEVER
1850

When one has had a fever, and the hair is falling off, take a tea-cupful of sage, steeped well in a quart of soft water; strain off into a tight bottle with an ounce of borax added.

FEVER AND AGUE
(Published in the *Austin City Gazette* the first newspaper published in Austin, Republic of Texas, Nov. 13, 1839)

The following simple recipe has never been known to fail, and is now published for the benefit of such as may be suffering under this disagreeable complaint:

1 oz. yellow peruvian bark	1 tbsp. pulverized cloves
1 oz. cream of tartar	1 pt. Teneriffe wine

Mix together, shake well, and take a wine glass full every two hours after the fever is off.

N. B. Butler taking the above — "a dram of Epsom salts or other med-
icines should be given to cleanse the stomach and render the cure more
speedy and certain." (N.Y. American).

☆　　☆　　☆

GROUCHY PERSON

Give a grouchy person a tea made of violet blossoms.

☆　　☆　　☆

HEADACHE CURE
1860

A cup of sour milk spread upon a thin cloth and applied to the
head will many times give relief. Or, a mustard plaster on the
back of the neck will often ease the pain.

★　　★　　★

One-half teaspoonful of the best ground ginger; as much soda as
will cover a three-cent piece. On this pour a wine glass full of
cold water; and drink.

HEART
1893

For heartburn mix 1 dram bicarbonate of soda, $1/2$ oz. powdered
rhubarb, 2 drams spirits of peppermint, and 4 oz. water. Dose: 1
tbsp. after meals.

★　　★　　★

For heart failure mix 10 cents worth of cloves, 10 cents worth of
cinnamon bark, pulverized. Put in a quart of pure whiskey and
take 1 to 3 times a day.

HICCUPS

Eat a teaspoon of peanut butter or boil a cup of dried apples in a
cup of water; drink juice while hot.

HOW TO KEEP WELL
1887

Don't sleep in a draught.
Don't go to bed with cold feet.
Don't stand over hot-air registers.
Don't eat what you do not need, just to save it.
Don't try to get cool too quickly after exercising.
Don't sleep in a room without ventilation of some kind.
Don't stuff a cold lest you should be next obliged
    to starve a fever.
Don't sit in a damp or chilly room without a fire.
Don't try to get along without flannel underclothing
    in winter.

INGROWING TOENAILS
1824 — Humphrey Jackson

Cut a notch in the center of the nail, or scrape it thin in the middle. Put a small piece of tallow in a spoon and heat it over a lamp until it becomes very hot. Drop two or three drops between the nail and granulation. The pain and tenderness will soon be relieved, and in a few days the granulation will be gone. One or two applications will cure the most obstinate case.

ITCH
1817 — Nancy Twomey

Use blood root, pulverized and steeped in strong apple vinegar, to make as strong as can be made, applied 3-4 times a day.

[Nancy Twomey came to Texas in 1835 from Georgia.]

KIDNEY AND BLADDER

Put 4 teaspoons each of horsetail grass and kidney wort into a pint of water and boil down to ½ pint. Drink ½ cupful at night just before retiring.

★ ★ ★

Eat 1 or 2 pokeberries a day for a couple of days.

LINAMENT
1900

Use a quart bottle. Put in 1 pint of cold water. Add:

2 oz. turpentine and shake 5 minutes

2 oz. of stronger ammonia and shake 5 minutes

1 egg broken and shake hard 5 minutes

2 oz. of spirits camphor and shake 5 minutes

Be sure to add ingredients as listed and shake full 5 minutes each time. If short the full quart, add enough cold water to fill and be sure to shake. Allow yourself full 20 minutes to make this up. Do not set aside; continue to mix and shake as directed as any other method will cause linament to curdle or to separate.

MUSTARD
1840

Mustard is another valuable remedy. No family should be without it. Two or three teaspoonfuls of ground mustard stirred into a half pint of water acts as an emetic very promptly, and is milder and easier to take than salt and water. Equal parts of ground mustard and flour or meal, made into a paste with warm water, and spread on a thin piece of muslin with another piece of muslin laid over it, forms the often indispensable mustard plaster. It is almost a specific for colic, when applied for a few minutes over the pit of the stomach. For all internal pains and congestions, there is no remedy of such great utility. Mix mustard with white of an egg to prevent blistering.

NEURALGIA
1840 — Taken from Grandmother Matthews's Scrapbook

I mention this illness that I may tell you how easily I was cured. I was bent double. I could not breathe. My physician told me to take a flat-iron and heat it as hot as I could bear, put a double

fold of flannel on the painful part, and move the iron to and fro on the flannel. I was cured as if by enchantment. My doctor told me that sometime since, a professor in one of our colleges, after suffering some days with neuralgia in the head, which he himself had tried to cure, sent for the former, who prescribed a hot flat-iron. The next time the doctor saw the professor, the latter exclaimed: "I had no sooner applied the heated iron to my head than instantly all pain had vanished."

ONION USAGE
1856 — Asa Wright and John Lloyd Halliburton families

A raw onion eaten for supper often prevents wakefulness at night.

Sliced roasted onions bound on the feet are useful in breaking up a cold or fever.

Sliced raw onions placed in rooms where there are fever or smallpox patients, and changed every few hours, absorb much of the poison. Burn the onions immediately.

The daily use of onions is said to prevent dysentery and fever.

Onions mashed fine and applied at once to a snakebite will draw the poison from the wound. The onions should be raw in this case and removed at short intervals. The poison will show green on the poultice.

To remove onion odor from the breath, eat parsley and vinegar; from the hands, rub them with celery.

PAIN ERADICATORS
1890

For toothache, headache, neuralgia, rheumatism, cramps and billiousness, colic, colds, coughs, and all female weaknesses: alcohol, 1 qt.; gum of camphor, 1 oz.; turpentine, 2 oz.; oil of cinnamon, 1 oz.; oil of spike, 1 oz.; tinct of capsicum, 3 oz.; chloroform, 2 oz.; oil cloves, 1 oz.; oil sassafras, 1 oz.; oil wintergreen, 1/2 oz.; powder capsicum, 2 oz.

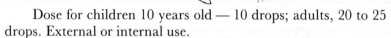

Dose for children 10 years old — 10 drops; adults, 20 to 25 drops. External or internal use.

Have a druggist to fill any quantity you wish, 2-3 ounces or any amount you desire to have, because he has to proportion the ingredients.

POISON ANTIDOTE

A standing antidote for poison by dew, poison oak, ivy, etc., is to take a handful of quicklime, dissolve in water, let it stand half an hour, then paint the poisoned parts with it. Three or four applications will never fail to cure the most aggravated cases. Poison from bees, hornets, spider bites, etc., is instantly arrested by the application of equal parts of common salt and bicarbonate of common soda well rubbed in on the place bitten or stung.

★ ★ ★

Poison of almost any kind swallowed will be instantly thrown from the stomach by drinking half a glass of water (warm is best), in which has been stirred a tablespoonful of ground mustard. As soon as vomiting ceases, drink a cup of strong coffee, into which has been stirred the white of an egg. This nullifies any remnant which the mustard might have left.

PYORRHEA
(Written in back of Grandmother Raven's cookbook — original source unknown.)

A half-pint of coal oil and two tablespoons of sulphur, used twice daily as a mouthwash, will cure pyorrhea.

RHEUMATISM
1807 — Hannah Elizabeth Hall Denny

Lemon juice is recommended as a certain cure for acute rheumatism. It is given in quantities of a tablespoon to twice the quantity of cold water, with sugar, every hour. The effect of the lemon juice is almost instantaneous.

★ ★ ★

Drink a mixture of honey, vinegar, and whiskey.

★ ★ ★

Drink powdered rhubarb dissolved in white whiskey.

RINGWORM

Make a strong solution of tobacco leaves and apply to affected area until it entirely disappears.

★ ★ ★

Tear a strip of paper from white bond and burn in a white saucer or plate. Wipe up yellow stain left in saucer with finger and apply to ringworm. Do this night and morning for 2 or 3 days. The ringworm will be cured.

SNAKE AND SPIDER BITES
1845

Put a few drops of pure carbolic acid on the bite, bathe with coal oil mixed with soda.

★ ★ ★

Cover with common baking soda; as it absorbs the poison and turns green, rub off lightly and replace with new. Repeat until soda no longer turns green.

★ ★ ★

Beat onions and salt together, wet tobacco, mix thoroughly. Split wound and apply at once.

SOFT CORN REMOVAL
1824 — Humphrey Jackson

Take a piece of lemon, cut it so as to let the toe through, and put the pulp next to the corn. Two or three applications will cure. Soft corns between the toes may be cured by a weak solution of carbolic acid.

[Humphrey Jackson arrived in Texas in 1824 with the original 300 Austin colonists.]

159

SORE THROAT GARGLE
1886 — Nancy Elizabeth Standifer Davis

Steep 1 medium-sized red pepper in ½ pt. of water, strain, and add ¼ pt. of good vinegar and a heaping teaspoonful each of salt and pulverized alum. Gargle with it as often as needed.

SORES
1895

Powdered alum is good for canker sores in the mouth; dusted in shoes it is good for feet that perspire freely.

Don't ever burn the cloth bandage from a sore; you must bury it for the sore to heal.

SPRAINED ANKLE

Moisten brown paper in vinegar. Wrap this around ankle. Elevate foot.

SPRAINS

A good lotion for a sprain is camphorated spirit, common vinegar, spirits of turpentine — 1 oz. of each.

TAPE WORM CURE
1886

Pumpkin seed, 1 oz., white sugar, ½ oz. (seed pounded fine and mixed with the sugar). A teaspoonful of the mixture every 2 hours, till all is taken. Follow the last dose with castor oil and spirits of turpentine.

TOO MUCH WATER
1860

Men and women are always going to extremes. Formerly, people did not bathe enough. Many persons who had gotten beyond "swimming" as a pastime were equally beyond all thought

of a thorough bath. Then the shower bath came into use, and the steambath, and Turkish bath, and the water-cure, and any amount of semi-scientific preaching on the vital importance of keeping the skin clean.

The consequence has been absurd notions on the subject, and a harmful practice. Not a few weak women must have their bath once, and in some cases, twice a day, through the year, and the habit has become so strong that they are uneasy if they do not indulge it.

Some persons have an idea that the perspiration could not get through the pores if they didn't daily scrub off the "dead skin." The fact is the pores are so numerous — nearly 3,000 in every square inch — that the perspiration passes through any ordinary dirt, as water does through coarse sand. Moreover, there is a force behind it which brings it out, as water in a spring is forced up through the earth. Some of the tribes of Africa, who habitually smear themselves with grease and utterly avoid water, are at least as healthy as we are.

The late Dr. Hall's journal contains many sensible articles. In a recent number is one against this over-doing with water. Twice a week, it says, is enough. "Too frequent bathing removes the oil with which nature covers the body, and which is so essential to health, and wears away the scarf-skin, and thus exposes too much of the network of nerves which terminate just below it."

Let one keep decently clean, and nature will look after the rest. A frequent change of the underclothing is as important as bathing. Where there is a bad odor from the body, it is often the case that some of the internal organs are not doing their work, and that medical advice is needed.

TOOTHACHE REMEDY

The large-leaved plantain of the door-yard is said to be a sure remedy for the toothache. The leaves are chopped finely, packed closely in a bottle, and covered with strong alcohol for a week. With this tincture a piece of cotton or wool is saturated and the

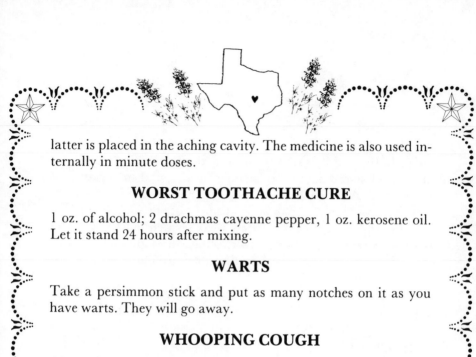

latter is placed in the aching cavity. The medicine is also used internally in minute doses.

WORST TOOTHACHE CURE

1 oz. of alcohol; 2 drachmas cayenne pepper, 1 oz. kerosene oil. Let it stand 24 hours after mixing.

WARTS

Take a persimmon stick and put as many notches on it as you have warts. They will go away.

WHOOPING COUGH

A cure for whooping cough: A teaspoonful of castor oil to a teaspoonful of molasses. Give a teaspoonful of the mixture whenever the cough is troublesome. It will afford relief at once, and in a few days will effect a cure. The same medicine relieves the croup, however violent the attack.

Conversion Charts

☆   ☆   ☆

WOMEN'S WORK

The old couplet, "Man's work, from sun to sun, Women's work is never done" is illustrated by the declaration of a housekeeper as to the amount of work she did in one department of housekeeping during the last year. She has made and baked 1,038 loaves of bread, 421 pies, 152 loaves of cake, 105 puddings, and 2,140 doughnuts. She has cooked 2,000 pounds of meat, 100 bushels of potatoes, takes care of the milk and butter of five cows, and looked after the thousand and one things which require attention from the housekeeper.

☆   ☆   ☆

TABLE OF WEIGHTS AND MEASURES

1901

60 drops = 1 teaspoon
3 teaspoons = 1 tablespoon
2 tablespoons = 1 liquid
   ounce
4 tablespoons = ¼ cup
16 tablespoons = 1 cup
1 wine glass = ¼ cup
¼ pint = 1 gill
2 cups = 1 pint
2 pints = 1 quart
4 quarts = 1 gallon
8 quarts = 1 peck
4 pecks = 1 bushel
16 ounces = 1 pound
4 cups flour = 1 pound
3 cups cornmeal = 1 pound

2 cups granulated sugar = 1
   pound
3½ cups confectioners sugar,
   sifted = 1 pound
2¼ cups brown sugar, firmly
   packed = 1 pound
2 cups solid meat = 1 pound
9 medium-sized eggs = 1
   pound
5 whole eggs = 1 cup
8-10 egg whites = 1 cup
13-14 egg yolks = 1 cup
2 cups solid butter = 1 pound
2 tablespoons butter = 1
   ounce

WEIGHTS AND MEASURES

Ten eggs equal one pound. Of brown sugar, one pound two ounces is one quart. Powdered sugar — one pound one ounce is one quart. Loaf sugar broken — one pound is one quart. Butter, when soft — one pound is one quart. Indian meal — one pound two ounces is one quart. Wheat flour — one pound is one quart.

From Then to Now

CONVERSIONS

The old ways of measuring ingredients, oven heat, and even size and type of ingredients were substantially different from modern thermostats, size of eggs and other products, and types of ingredients available in modern times. These conversion charts will help to convert old recipes to modern usage.

1. Eggs were much smaller than modern-day large eggs. Small eggs should always be used with old recipes.

2. When the recipe says "butter the size of an egg," compare it to a *small egg* or use about two tablespoons of butter.

3. There was no cake flour and all the baking was done with common flour. Many times cooks mixed corn starch with the flour.

4. There was no refined white sugar. The sugar was more like our light brown sugar.

Baking

Names given to the various temperature stages for baking:

Slow oven .... 250 degrees to 325 degrees F.
Moderately slow oven .... 326 degrees to 349 degrees F.
Moderate oven .... 350 degrees to 375 degrees F.
Moderately hot oven .... 376 degrees to 399 degrees F.
Hot oven .... 400 degrees to 449 degrees F.
Quick oven .... 450 degrees to 500 degrees F.
Very hot oven .... 501 degrees to 575 degrees F.

Measurements

1 cup flour = 4 ounces
4 cups of flour = 1 pound
$3^{1}/_{4}$ cups whole wheat flour = 1 pound
1 tablespoon butter = $^{1}/_{2}$ ounce
1 cup butter = 8 ounces
1 sq. unsweetened chocolate = 1 ounce
1 square grated unsweetened chocolate = $5^{1}/_{2}$ tbsp.
1 pound raisins = $2^{2}/_{3}$ cups
1 pound dates = $2^{1}/_{2}$ cups
1 pound figs (chopped) = 3 cups
1 pound walnuts (chopped) = $3^{1}/_{2}$ cups
1 pinch = $^{1}/_{8}$ tsp.
60 drops = 1 tsp.
3 tsp. = 1 tbsp.
2 tbsp. = 1 fluid oz.
$^{1}/_{2}$ cup solid butter = $^{1}/_{4}$ lb.

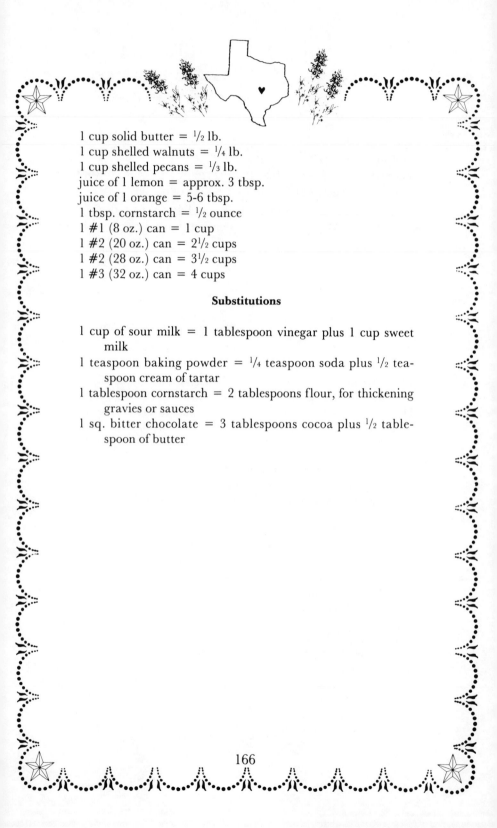

1 cup solid butter = $^{1}/_{2}$ lb.
1 cup shelled walnuts = $^{1}/_{4}$ lb.
1 cup shelled pecans = $^{1}/_{3}$ lb.
juice of 1 lemon = approx. 3 tbsp.
juice of 1 orange = 5-6 tbsp.
1 tbsp. cornstarch = $^{1}/_{2}$ ounce
1 #1 (8 oz.) can = 1 cup
1 #2 (20 oz.) can = $2^{1}/_{2}$ cups
1 #2 (28 oz.) can = $3^{1}/_{2}$ cups
1 #3 (32 oz.) can = 4 cups

Substitutions

1 cup of sour milk = 1 tablespoon vinegar plus 1 cup sweet
    milk
1 teaspoon baking powder = $^{1}/_{4}$ teaspoon soda plus $^{1}/_{2}$ tea-
    spoon cream of tartar
1 tablespoon cornstarch = 2 tablespoons flour, for thickening
    gravies or sauces
1 sq. bitter chocolate = 3 tablespoons cocoa plus $^{1}/_{2}$ table-
    spoon of butter

Translations

Baking Soda is the familiar bicarbonate of soda, and was called for in the old recipes either to act as a leavening agent in baking or to prevent curdling of milk and tomato dishes, or to provide an aerated texture to such confections as brittle candies. Until the middle 1800s, baking soda was elegantly called "saleratus" and combined with the acidity of buttermilk and sour cream or milk, or such sweeteners as molasses for making quick breads.

Sour milk and cream were natural and staple ingredients in the old kitchen, and buttermilk came directly from the churn.

Saleratus see baking soda.

Spiders were cherished items in the old kitchen. It is nothing more mysterious than a capacious frying pan, preferably of cast iron, in which things fry or simmer or keep warm in a wonderfully satisfactory manner.

"Back of the stove" is an expression known to all old-time cooks who used huge black iron wood ranges with plenty of space away from the fire box to let things finish cooking slowly and gently. The warming oven of such a stove is ideal for drying mittens, etc., between meals. With double boilers and trivets it is possible to achieve the same slow cooking process on a modern gas or electric stove. The present-day saying "it's cooking on the back burner" must have derived from this custom.

Contributors

DRT Chapters from District VIII providing recipes and other material for this book:

Baron de Bastrop Chapter, Bastrop
Abishai Mercer Dickson Chapter, Seguin
Gonzales Chapter, Gonzales
Ferdinand Lindheimer Chapter, New Braunfels
Martin Wells Chapter, Round Rock
Moon-McGehee Chapter, San Marcos
Monument Hill Chapter, La Grange
Llano Chapter, Llano
Cornelius Smith Chapter, Luling
Texian Chapter, Austin
William Barret Travis Chapter No. 3, Austin
Reuben Hornsby, Austin

Baron de Bastrop Chapter

Kathleen Arnold
Gladys Birdwell
Mary Ann Bryant
Ruth Ann Bryant
Alyce Ferguson
Margaret Hanna
Vanessa Huffine
Valerie Johnson
Martha Lambert
Loretta Lernhardt
JoNell Majors
Agnes McWhorter
Martha Redford
Elberta Schultz
Ruth Smith
Kay Valenta
Kathleen Wesr
Evelyn Wolf

Abishai Mercer Dickson Chapter

SEBASTOPOL 1850-1855

ABISHAI MERCER DICKSON Chapter GUADALUPE COUNTY 1969

SEGUIN PECAN   N. N.

Mrs. F. W. Batey (Olivia)
Mrs. Jim Benson (Florine)
Mrs. Jack Brady (Sue)
Mrs. F. W. Brandenberger
  (Marjorie)
Mrs. J. M. Cowley (Lois)
Mrs. E. W. Darilek (Lucille)
Mrs. Virgil Halm (Maxine)
Mrs. Oscar Huber (Velma)
Mrs. Franklin Hurt (Katie Lay)
Mrs. Phillip Jones (Betty Jean)
Mrs. William Koehler (Anna Bell)

Mrs. Maynard Kolb (Helen)
Mrs. Gilbert Nagel (Elsie)
Mrs. Roland Naumann (Nora)
Mrs. Albert I. Orr (Mary Louise)
Mrs. Earl Rives (June)
Mrs. Raymond Scheider (Aline)
Mrs. R. K. Shafer (Gertrude)
Mrs. Raymond Spahn (Doris)
Mrs. T. H. Terry (Mildred)
Mrs. Henry Timmermann (Katie)
Mrs. Casper Traeger (Ollie)

Gonzales Chapter

Lady Ona Adkisson
Amanda Anderson
Mrs. J. C. Barfield (Louise)
Mrs. Robert Boothe (Florence)
Mrs. Ross Boothe (Lucille)
Mrs. James Bussey (Delores)
Mrs. Charles Chenault (Carey)
Mrs. Louis Cleveland (Alta)
Mrs. Rufus Collins (Audrey)
Mrs. Vernon Crozier (Laura)
Mrs. Bryan Denman (Ruth)
Mrs. J. C. Dilworth, Jr. (Hercel)
Mrs. David Dworaczyk (Robbie)
Mrs. Rufus Floyd (Raguet)
Mrs. David Glover (Susan)
Mrs. Frank Glover (Ola)
Mrs. Italia Graham
Mrs. B. Gray (Vivian)
Mrs. Raymond Gray (Dorothy)
Rosannah Green
Mrs. Thomas Gregg (Maude)
Mrs. W. F. Gustafson (Margaret)

Mrs. W. R. Hendershot, Sr.
  (Patsy)
Marjorie Hyatt
Mrs. Matthew Jacobs (Melissa)
Mary Jahnke
Mrs. Carlton Jordan (Sandra)
Mrs. Russell Kreutzer (Rachel)
Mrs. James Lewis (Eva)
Mrs. Fain McDougal
Mrs. Berthold Nowotny (Wilma)
Mrs. Hobson Parker (Larue)
Mrs. Clay Pope (Mary)
Mrs. Perry Rayes (Margaret)
Mrs. Tom Read (Katie)
Mrs. Charles Richardson (Jo Ann)
Mrs. James Scott (Margaret)
Mrs. Ray Shanklin (Mary)
Mrs. Clate Thorn (Lottie)
Mrs. Robert Vackar (Edna)
Mrs. Henry Vollentine (Genevieve)
Mrs. Faye Walker
Mrs. J. W. Waters (Rosemary)

Ferdinand Lindheimer Chapter

Mrs. Fred Adams (Diane)
Mrs. Carolyn Appling
Mrs. Perry Barker (Sudie)
Mrs. W. T. Barron (Julia)
Mrs. Thomas Burrell (Kathryn)
Mrs. S. T. Burrus (Ann)
Mary Ellis Burrus
Mrs. Michael Byrd (Lynne)
Mrs. Edward Campbell (Dorothy)
Mrs. Blayne Council (Vicki)
Mrs. George Cuming (Valerie)
Mrs. Christopher Deasy (Kimberly)
Mrs. Charles Edison (Amy)
Mrs. William Ellis (Ruth)
Mrs. Tristram Englehardt (Beulah)
Mrs. Ray Felger (Jeannette)
Mrs. E. P. Fulton (Lora)
Mrs. John Gerhardt (Esther)
Mrs. Guy Greer (Ella)
Mrs. Agnes Grimm
Mrs. J. Edwin Grimm (Mary Ann)
Mrs. Steve Hain (Cynthia)
Mrs. Jean-Claude Hand (Candy)
Mrs. Calvin Henley, Jr. (Linda Sue)
Mrs. Florian Holm (Marie)
Mrs. Mattie Howard
Mrs. Viola Johns

Mrs. Elliott Johnson (Minnie)
Mrs. Forrest Johnson (Edith)
Mrs. John Kimple (Shelia)
Mrs. Richard Klemmedson (Carolyn)
Mrs. John Long (Linda Jean)
Mrs. Robert Lozo, Sr. (Mary Elizabeth)
Mrs. Carl Martin (Edna)
Mrs. Joseph Mitchell, Jr. (Verily)
Lucy Marie Mitchell
Mrs. Robert Moore (Joyce)
Mrs. William Morris (Jeannette)
Mrs. Donald Offerman (Ida)
Mrs. Erwin Proud (Luciclaire)
Mrs. Curt Schmidt (Sarah)
Mrs. Ted Schoch (Mary Jane)
Mrs. Linton Smith (Margaret)
Mrs. Michael Spain (Bette Lu)
Mrs. Kent Stevens (Cynthia Ann)
Mrs. Ernest Stevenson (Mabel)
Mrs. K. N. Talaat (Amanda)
Mrs. Corine Thomas
Mrs. Charles Turner (Sandra)
Mrs. Dennie Ware (Barbara Jean)
Mrs. Brownwyn Anne Wilson
Jeanne Wilson

Martin Wells Chapter

Mary Clampitt Aston
Margaret Duncan Ball
E. Bunnie Louise Brooks
Winnie F. Bell Brown
Rachel Asher Bryson
Mary Bettye Clampitt
Mary Smith Craddock
Ruth Jenkins Curley
Beulah L. Hoffman Dannelley
Margaret JoAnn Nettles Diskin
Faye O. Darby Duncan
Sharon K. Orr Duncan
Tylene McGregor Edmiston
Erma J. Kingery Ellison
Willie R. Asher Foerster
Michelle Robertson Frizzell
Barbara G. James Fuller
Katharine L. Baring Fuller
Mary Louise Fuller
Vanessa Louise Fuller
Patricia J. Edmundson Gaines
Sylvia F. Mitchell Goodson
Jean L. Moss Goulding
Dr. Peggy M. Goulding
Mary Jane Nettles Hammack
Ruby J. Murray Harris
Jacque Hawkins
Jo Jodie Johnson Henry
Sherry J. Kirk Houston
Verna F. Hall Jansen
Gladys Hanks Johnson

Helen Murray Johnson
Nancy C. Devlin Kelly
Mary L. Hinde Mayhew
Rachel A. Bryson McAllister
Ina C. Bell McLendon
Betty M. Melde
Suzanne Gibson Mogonye
Nora G. Johnson Myers
Penny M. R. Harmon Myers
Phyllis L. Tuma Neves
Diane L. Billingsley Parker
Peggy J. Bell Phillips
Billie L. Bryson Price
Ester C. Stewart Rogers
Dorothy M. Stallings
Willie D. Stallings
Rosalind M. Miller Stoba
Dixie D. Benton Stucky
Nadine Ferrell Sutton
Barbara S. Miller Tew
Lora L. Baring Thomas
Frances E. Mason Thompson
Karen R. Dannelly Thompson
Katherine R. Thompson
Anna Reavis Tomlinson
Frances I. Ferrell Varan
Vesta Cochran White
Mary W. Stuart-McAskill Wiggins
Dayne C. Benson Wright
Willa J. Smith Zimmerman

Moon-McGehee Chapter

Mrs. Robert Bowden (Vera)
Mrs. Billy Boyd (Ginger)
Mrs. Davis Burgum (Gaytha)
Mrs. Carol Burton (Carrie)
Mrs. Darrell Butler (Brenda)
Mrs. Mary Jane Denney
Mrs. Henry Dettman (Roberta)
Mrs. G. W. Dickey (Madaline)
Mrs. Fred Feltner (Lydia)
Mrs. Charles Hall (Anita)
Mrs. Alex Johnson (Gretchen)
Mrs. Samuel Johnson (Alice)
Mrs. Jan Kasaw (Alice)
Mrs. Glen Maley (Kittie)

Mrs. Doyal Milner (Mary)
Mrs. Carroll Moench (Lois)
Mrs. Eugene Morrow (Alene)
Mrs. Kay Mullican
Mrs. Carroll Parman (Carolyn)
Mrs. Lewis Parr (Reed)
Mrs. Orvel Perkins (Michelle)
Mrs. Richard Phillips (Virginia)
Mrs. Robert Pruett (Susan)
Mrs. G. A. Schulle (Gladys)
Mrs. Hershel Walling (Maude)
Mrs. Charles Wiegand (Josephine)
Mrs. Wayne Windle (Janice)
Mrs. Wilton Woods (Virginia)
Mrs. William Wyatt (Tula)

Monument Hill Chapter

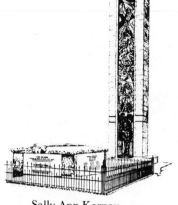

Dorothy Wallace Albrecht
Laurie Fay Albrecht
Julia Stuesser Anderson
Kathleen Stuesser Baldwin
Elizabeth Fietsam Bean
Debora Fietsam Behlen
Cindy Baldwin Crawford
Ruby Matthews Darnell
Sadie Wallace Dietzel
Lillian Stuermer Dyer
Diana Fietsam
Kathryn Barkley Fischer
Mary Mueller Frank
Cynthia Karnau Garbus
Deborah Belk Higgins
Glenn Denise Higgins
Betty Phillips Hill
Doris Bean Hoffman
Mary Oldfield Jackson
L. Christine Dyer Jervis
Rox Ann Albrecht Johnson
Eileen Frank Karnau

Sally Ann Karnau
Dawn Keilers
Elva Meiners Keilers
Grace Matthews Kocurek
Bridget Bean Luther
Sarah Peel Mabry
I. Carolyn Calvin Marble
Jana Fischer McLain
Beatrice Hagemann Meiners
Marilyn Frank Miller
Joan Marie Phillips
Mattie Taylor Phillips
Jennifer Placke
Claudean Leyendecker Saunders
Darlene Stancik
Joyce Matthews Stancik
Lillian Fietsam Stuesser
Maria Stuesser
Merle Jean Jenkins Thornton
E. LaDoris Doughty Weber
Deena Higgins Wenske
Imogene Fietsam Williams

Llano Chapter

Mrs. Donald Bass (Sylvia)
Mrs. Vernon Bonnet (Betty)
Mrs. John Bourke (Nettie)
Mrs. Royce Cheatham (Edna)
Mrs. Denman Christopher
 (Geraldine)
Mrs. James Cook (Jo Ann)
Mrs. George Daltwas (Jean)
Mrs. Jennings Day (Martha)
Mrs. Sidney Elliott (Alline)
 (Sidney deceased)
Mrs. Webster Fowler (Lillian)
Mrs. Jack Hahn (Geneva)
Mrs. Stanley Hanson (Elaine)
Mrs. Vernon Harper, Jr. (Sharon)
Mrs. John Horton (Lelah)
Mrs. Keith Howell (Brenda)
Mrs. Joseph Jackson (Muriel)
Mrs. Larry Jensen (Shirley)
Mrs. Cletus Kleen (Betty Jo)

Mrs. John McBride (Joan)
Mrs. Robert McMullen (Billie)
Mrs. Frank Meine, Jr.
 (Vina Mae)
Mrs. Rex Michel (Joy)
Mrs. William Miller (Carmen)
Mrs. Charles Nicholson (Martha)
Mrs. Egon Parkington (Margaret)
Mrs. Kelli Nicholson Shandera
Mrs. Herbert Stehle (Vivian)
Mrs. Era Teel (Ella Jean)
Mrs. Murrell Terry (Helen)
Mrs. Geneva Tetley
Mrs. Thomas Thurmond (Carolyn)
Hope Tinney
Mrs. Dor Tinney (Leola)
Mrs. Jack Van Horn (Jane)
Mrs. Ronnie Vineyard (Sydna)
Mrs. John Wade, Jr. (Evelyn)
Mrs. Clarence Wilson (Imogene)
Joan Wilson

Cornelius Smith Chapter

Mrs. Lennie Mae Baker
Mrs. Marylee Bolles
Mrs. Sandra Deanne Cain
Blackstone
Mrs. Dorothy Nell Ivey Cain
Mrs. Sharron Dianne Cain Clayton
Mrs. Patricia Louise Fogle Crisler
Mrs. Lorraine Ellis Crockett
Mrs. Ople Liddie Colwell Crowell
Mrs. Alice Abigail McGaffey Frazier
Mrs. Linda Lanay Frazier Gabbert
Mrs. Vivian McShan Gray
Mrs. Francis Inez Froh Griffin
Mrs. Linda Kay Hurt Halliburton
Mrs. Gladys Joy Daniels Hanson
Mrs. Patsy Evelyn Jones Hendershot
Mrs. Iantha Maxine Moses
Henderson
Mrs. Carolyn Virginia Ellis Hilburn
Mrs. Julie Kate Crockett Howell

Mrs. Nancy Carole Frazier Hughes
Mrs. Lillie Johanna Eiband Kollert
Mrs. Carolyn Lea McCullock Leet
Donna Gayle Lightsey
Mrs. Judith Kay Millican Lightsey
Mrs. Letha Mae Linscomb Lorenz
Mrs. Mary Elizabeth McGaffey
Manning
Mrs. Gertrude Lucille Linscomb
Millican
Mrs. Ruby Lee Linscomb Mueller
Mrs. Mamie Jane Moses Nickells
Mrs. Corinne Marie Pierce Philley
Mrs. Edna Mae Ivey Recknor
Cheryl Lyn Smith
Rev. Linda Margaret Watkins Smith
Mrs. Muriel Smith Turner
Mrs. Madeline Maxine Watkins
Westbrook
Mrs. Andra Pierson White
Mrs. Peggy Irma Paine Wood

Texian Chapter

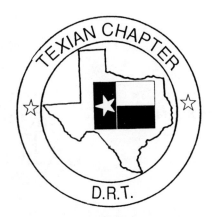

Carol Raven Adams
Hazel Houston Angus
Nellie Holman Bartlett
Allene Munlin Berwick
Judith Morehead Chapin
Carol June Christian
Helen Harper Clarke
Pat Cloud
Vaughn Dane Craft
Elinor Pantermuehl Crisswell
Anna Secrest Fell
Elizabeth C. Flynn
Gethrel Arlon Franke
Rachel Magill Gholson
Mary Carrington Gowen
Patt Lel Griffin

Lel Purcell Hawkins
Billie Connell Jordan
Rowena Darter Looney
Betty Raven Martin
Anna Lancaster Mertz
Judith English Morehead
Pansy Nichols
Willard Griffith Nitschke
Ann Pollard
Margaret Howze Purcell
Esther Altgelt Riske
Elizabeth Stoneham Rogers
Catherine Hall Schwartz
Marie Davis Smith
Karen Lee Tweedy
Hazel Henderson Wright

William Barret Travis Chapter No. 3

Active Members:
Mrs. Helen A. Altman
Cleo Arnett
Mrs. J. R. Barlow
Caroline Boales Bass
Mrs. L. M. Bowers
Mrs. M. H. Brannen
Mrs. H. Brown
Mrs. W. Bugg
Mrs. H. E. Cadwallader
Mrs. J. T. Carlson
Mrs. E. J. Castille
Mrs. K. L. Clapham
Mrs. M. H. Coleman
Mrs. A. J. Connally
Mrs. R. V. Conner
Mrs. Sam G. Cook
Mrs. D. G. Cooke
Maria Celeste Costley
Mary G. Crain
Mrs. L. B. Cunningham
Mrs. C. F. Debarbrie
Mrs. R. Dolhof
Dawn C. East
Mrs. P. Emmert
Andrea M. Fedor
Rosalie Ann Fedor
Mrs. S. Fedor

Mary B. Fleischer
M. C. Forister
Mrs. D. R. Gage
Mrs. N. A. Giblin
Mrs. G. Glober
Mrs. W. H. Goines
Mrs. J. B. Golden
Mrs. G. P. Goudreau
Phyllis M. Green
Mrs. J. S. Green
Mrs. F. T. Hankey, Jr.
Mrs. G. L. Hardin
Sharon A. Hardin
Mrs. L. B. Harding
Mrs. J. L. Hill
Mrs. Clyde C. Holder, Jr.
Mrs. G. F. Hollis
Mrs. T. W. Hollis
Mrs. L. M. Igo
Mrs. M. Jackson
Mrs. W. G. Jackson
Mrs. H. E. Johnson
Pamela S. Johnson
Mrs. B. W. Larson, Sr.
Mrs. T. C. Leshikar, Jr.
Dr. Robin H. Lock
Mrs. E. L. Lundelius
Mrs. Lola L. Marcellus

Mrs. R. C. McAnelly
Mrs. Ethel McCutcheon
Mrs. E. A. McDonald
Mrs. H. E. Mecredy, Jr.
Mrs. T. E. Mellett
Mrs. J. L. Merritt
Mrs. R. S. Miller
Edna Maree Moore
Mrs. J. F. Morgan
Helen C. Munds
Mrs. C. F. Niebuhr
Mrs. Lois Smith Nulty
Mrs. J. B. Pace
Mrs. Trya Kay Peterson
Mrs. M. W. Plumb
Ila Mae Poe
Mrs. F. Polk
Mrs. J. W. Preston
Mrs. R. H. Rade
Mrs. L. A. Raeke
Mrs. A. Ramirez
Mrs. R. C. Redfield
Mrs. J. W. Reed
Mrs. E. W. Richardson
Mrs. Charlie Ross
Mrs. F. E. Ryals, Jr.
Mrs. G. Sandlin
Mrs. J. H. Schorr
Mrs. J. D. Seals
Mrs. W. B. Shipp
Mrs. John R. Singleton
Mrs. M. M. Smiland
Mrs. Clyde Smith
Mrs. Kenneth Smith
Mrs. Noble E. Smith
Mrs. D. E. Sponberg
Mrs. Martha Stansbury
Mrs. Roy Starnes
Ellagene Towns Stenger
Mrs. Charles Taylor
Mrs. Delma C. Thames
Demp Toney
Mrs. Jo Tuttle

Mrs. H. A. Underwood
Mrs. R. C. Walker
Mrs. G. C. West
Mrs. W. L. Wheelock
Mrs. L. V. Wilkinson
Mrs. U. P. Williams
Mrs. Wm. R. Young
Nonactive Members:
Mrs. K. W. Abood
Mrs. Stephen Arnold
Mrs. L. L. Bennett
Mrs. E. E. Brogren
Mrs. B. W. Butler
Mrs. J. B. Chiodo
Mrs. B. L. Chote
Mrs. Mildred Couser
Mrs. R. W. Cunningham
Mrs. Price Daniel
Mrs. C. R. Daugherty
Mrs. J. S. Delaney
Mrs. Mabel H. Dingwall
Mrs. H. A. Dulan
Mrs. J. H. Duran
Mrs. A. C. Egg
Mrs. E. P. Gill
Mrs. Neal D. Johnson
Mrs. J. G. Kaufmann
Mrs. D. T. Koontz
Mrs. J. Lentini
Betty J. R. Marschall
Myreta Matthews
Mrs. T. D. McGinty
Mrs. J. J. McMaster
Virginia Mecredy
Mrs. R. B. Miller
Mrs. C. C. Munds
Mrs. D. R. Murray
Lula Earl Owens
Mrs. J. L. Placke
Mrs. Henrietta Preece
Lillian Rabb
Mrs. W. J. Redwine
Mrs. R. L. Reeves

179

Mary T. Rickert
Mrs. R. G. Rickert
Mrs. M. R. Riggin
Mrs. W. Rossman
Mrs. T. W. Sarytchoff

Mrs. D. B. Stone
Mrs. J. W. Straiton
Mrs. H. T. Taylor
Mrs. H. Williams
Mrs. R. R. Williams

Reuben Hornsby Chapter

Mrs. W. P. Barber
Mrs. Chas. Barefield
Mrs. J. W. Browning
Mrs. Andrew Byers
Mrs. Pat Callahan
Mrs. J. P. Callan
Mrs. Perry A. Christianson
Carol Ann Dittlinger
Mrs. Richard Dolecek
Mrs. Joe Douglas
Mrs. Garland S. Foscue
Mrs. Chester Franklin
Vivien Leigh Franklin
Mrs. Ike David Hall
Mrs. Sarah S. Johnson
Mrs. Terry W. Kilpatrick
Mrs. Billy Gene Kleespies
Mrs. August Krumm, Jr.

Mrs. Dorothy Landoll
Mrs. Leon A. Mangum
Mrs. James B. Marley
Mrs. Dudley McCalla
Mrs. Michael H. McCloskey
Mrs. Steve Meeks
Mrs. Russell W. Meinardus
Mrs. Raymond P. Menges, Jr.
Mrs. Charles D. Patterson
Mrs. Wm. C. Pearce
Mrs. Will Platt, Jr.
Mrs. Wilna L. Sepulvdo
Mrs. Alan W. Shea
Mrs. Fred Slaughter
Mrs. W. E. Switzer
Claudia R. Upton
Laura Upton
Mrs. James E. Upton
Mrs. George W. Wilsin

Bibliography
(Partial)

Austin City Gazette (first newspaper published in Austin, Republic of Texas), November 13, 1839.

Dr. Chase's Recipes or Information for Everybody. 1900.

Dr. Chase's Recipes — Medicine Book. Treatment of Diseases. 30 Home Remedies. Publishing Date — November 28, 1886. Foreword by L. Davis, Secretary, Washtensaw County Pioneer Society, Ann Arbor, Michigan.

Civil War Diary, Handwritten by W. B. Gowen, 1864.

Dining Room and Kitchen. 1880.

Every Woman Her Own Cook. (Book very old and title page, etc., missing.)

First Texas Cookbook. By Auxiliary, First Presbyterian Church of Houston, Texas. 1883. Published in Texas. Republished in 1986 by Eakin Press. Foreword by Mary Faulk Koock.

"Godey's Lady's Book Magazine," Vol. L-14 (July-December, 1859).

Good Cooking. 1896.

Housekeeping in Old Virginia. By Marion Cabell Tyree, 1879.

"Ladies Temperance Union of Ozona, Texas" (handwritten cookbook). 1909.

Mary Randolph Cookbook, ca 1826. Virginia.

Matthews, Lella May McMillan Taylor. Recipe scrapbook, 1878.

Matthews, Nancy Leanorah. Scrapbooks containing news of the day from varied publications — dating to 1838.

McKenzie's Ten Thousand Receipts in all the Domestic Arts. October 1865.

Medicine Book, 1886.

The Model Cookbook. 1892 — date on spine; in the Beaty family for many years previous to that date.

The Modern Cookbook by Williard Griffith Nitschke, 1892.

New Settlement Cookbook. Simon & Schuster, 1901.

Old English Cookery.

The Picayunes Creole Cookbook. 1901.

Sears Roebuck Cookbook. 1800.

Texas Cookbook. Printed in Texas, 1883.

White House Cookbook, belonging to Katie Hurt's mother. 1887.

The Young Housekeeping's Friend. 1859.

Index

183

186